HONEST RUST AND GOLD

A SECOND COLLECTION OF PROSE AND POETRY

FRANCIS ETHEREDGE

En Route Books and Media, LLC
St. Louis, MO

⊕ENROUTE
Make the time

En Route Books and Media, LLC
5705 Rhodes Avenue
St. Louis, MO 63109

Cover credit: TJ Burdick

Library of Congress Control Number: 2020951074

ISBN-13: 978-1-952464-36-2

Contents

Acknowledgements

Having drafted the work as a whole and developed, with the help of prompts of one kind or another, the basic content and structure, a number of other people have contributed to the beginning and the end of the book as a whole and as a guest poet at the conclusion of each of the seven parts:

Bishop Fintan Monahan (Foreword) and John O'Brien, Frater, OFM, (End Word) and the following guest poets have contributed a piece of work at the end of each of the seven parts of the book: Ravi Shankar; Fr. Antoine Altieri; Richard Bowdery; Annabelle Moseley; Teresa J. Herbic; Dr. Mary Anne Urlakis, whose son Joseph has furnished his mother's work with accompanying photographs; and James Sale. However, there is one exception to this pattern in that Russell Rogers wrote a poem that is both definitely a part of the times in which we live and the questions that we ask; and, therefore, it has been included at the beginning of Part II: Awareness. I would also like to thank Helen Williams for both her proof reading and critical help; and, in the same capacity, the very helpful contributions of Kelly Jayne Lazell.

At the same time, however, a book without a publisher is a letter without an address; and, therefore, I wish to mention, as well, Dr. Sebastian Mahfood, OP, of En Route Books and Media, USA, for publishing this and other books and, of course, for Cambridge

Scholars Publishing four books in England.

So, with a great sense of gratitude to the generosity of the contributing authors and other collaborators, I wish to beg God to bless them and all who read these diverse words!

FOREWORD: BISHOP FINTAN MONAHAN OF KILLALOE DIOCESE, IRELAND

In his "Acknowledgement", Francis Etheredge, the author of this welcome volume, calls this work "a collection of diverse words". In his "Epilogue" he calls it "a coalescence of different impressions", "a dialogue between grace and nature", and also, an "awakening" of encouragement for so much that is good in the world, in people around us and in those who take the time to help us reflect on all that. This book is all of that and much more.

The great title of this work deserves reflection, *Honest Rust and Gold*. It has connotations of the scriptural reference from Matthew 13:52: *Then He said to them, "Therefore every scribe instructed concerning the kingdom of heaven is like a householder who brings out of his treasure things new and old."*

I welcome these "left-over" and "round-two" reflections of a scribe we are now familiar with and I am grateful for his reflections, tempered by the ravages of the rust of time-honoured and mature reflection but transformed into the gold that nourishes our spirits with the grace of the Good News of our faith.

The writer, a busy lay theologian and father of a large family, acknowledges in the "positive pull towards this work" the vocation of being a writer, what he calls the call to "transform a mass of words into a living sense" and crafting words to share and reflect on what is meaningful and worthwhile. He tells us that "maybe this book is like that moment of stepping out of the busyness of life in order to notice what is around us" and I certainly appreciate the wisdom between the two covers that does that in so many ways.

In the play by Brian Friel, *Philadelphia, here I come* there is an interesting dialogue between a young man called Gar and the local parish priest. Gar is disillusioned with the boredom, tedium and lack of opportunity of rural life of Ballybeg in Donegal in the 1960's. He is getting ready to emigrate to the US in search of excitement, adventure and meaning. The world he lives in has not been able to sustain him. The Church he subscribes to has not nourished his spirit. The text runs:

> "Gar lashes out at Canon Byrne. You could translate all this loneliness, this groping, this dreadful bloody buffoonery into Christian terms that will make life bearable for us all. And you don't say a word. Why arid Canon? Isn't this your job? To translate? Why don't you speak then? Prudence, arid Canon? Prudence, be damned! Christianity isn't prudent. It's insane!"

One of the big themes of Friel's work is the longing for institutions like the Church, or works of literature, to translate and make sense of the routine mundaneness of the world around us and the "insanity" of the Christian message. Francis Etheredge and his guest writers make a great effort to do that for us by continually going back to the wells of inspiration and faith. We need the work of such people to sustain and nourish us.

Great themes, emotions and states of being are explored in

Etheredge's prose and poetry. Things like life, existence, nature, good, evil, beginnings, awakenings, technology, nakedness, superficiality, sharing, sight, colour, news, flitting, soundings, boiling, vulnerability, loneliness, poverty, old age, infirmity, death, the afterlife, faith, the Sacraments, the life of Grace, the hope of the life and death of Jesus Christ and we are offered contemporary musings, too, on the holocaust and living with Covid-19.

I remember being at a poetry reading by Seamus Heaney, RIP, some years back, and while one might struggle to get the sense of what a poet is trying to convey from the bare text being read, hearing the narrative of the background of someone like Heaney and listening to the music of the poem as it is being read, gives so much more in grasping the experience of what the genre is conveying. The seamless combination of prose and poetry in this volume of Francis Etheredge and guests helps greatly to achieve that in *Honest Rust and Gold.*

This work is beautifully crafted in structure. My English teacher tried hard to drum into us at school, years ago, that our literary efforts need a beginning, a middle, and an end. This work takes that instruction seriously with the opening section entitled "Before" and the closing section "After". It reminds me of the parabola like journey of Philippians 2:6-11: the journey of Jesus Christ from above, to live in this world and return to heaven again.

In the Liturgy of the Hours, for Lauds, on one of the Saturday mornings there is a prayer of intercession that asks God's blessing on musicians, artists, poets and craftspeople. We need the artists and craftspeople of this world to help us step off the merry-go-round of our busy world, to go a little deeper and explore the meaning behind it all. It is all the more profound, in my view, when an artist can direct us to the bottom of a rainbow that contains, not a rusty piece of metal, but a crock of gold that is the Good News that Jesus Christ offers to us.

Francis Etheredge and his guests have done that for us in the words that follow. I hope you enjoy this pilgrim journey as much as I have.

✠ Fintan Monahan

Fintan Monahan is Bishop of Killaloe, based in Ennis, Co. Clare. He is author of *A Perfect Peace, Newman, Saint for Our Time* and has just completed a work on Thomas Merton, *Peace Smiles, Rediscovering Thomas Merton.* He is currently working on a similar work on CS Lewis and another volume on Pope Emeritus Benedict XVI.

GENERAL INTRODUCTION

The title to this book of prose and poetry has been slow in coming although, in between other work, at times I have noticed a positive pull towards it; and, as such, it remains to be seen whether this "attraction" will be like time disappearing into a "black hole" ever to be lost or, instead, it will be an investment in the process of writing another book because it is "there" to be written. Imagine, like the sculptor who looks at a piece of stone, a piece of wood or "found metal or object" and sees a possibility in the grain and blend of layers, in the shape and textured surface, to be cleaned or used, in the colors and discolorations left by weathering or other workmanship – that just as there is a meaning to be shelled or pointed up so there is a book breaking into the blank pages and driving the deliberations that transform a mass of words into living sense.

Scrapings or surprises

"The Second Collection", in a Church, is that collection which follows after people have put what they are going to give to the local work of God. Thus the sense of scraping together what is left to give could go either way. Either this title is a sign of running out of ideas or it is a sign of surprises still to come. So: Is this a book about what is left over? But it is almost impossible to give up doing what is unprofitable, not because profitability is not a purpose, but because the spring of words is unbounded by the practicalities of life. Alternatively, then, this book is a gift of going again to the well of opportunity and delving, so to speak, amidst the bits and pieces that had started to come together in a box of words, sometimes run through with a threading point and sometimes left, as it were, to grow through pondering to bursting into nothing or rubbed, alight, into a fuller form of itself.

Stopping to finish or to start afresh

Changes, then, either belong to the work itself or are foreign to the first thoughts but somehow gradually spawn an unforeseen development which, not like a cancer, grows amorphously before shedding what is irrelevant and standing clear as a word in its own right. Maybe this book is like that moment of stepping out of the busyness of life in order to notice what is around us. Thus it is not so much about where a person is, although it has been possible to be beside the Grand Canyon, to be in the underground passages wherein singing was both embarrassing and beautiful or to be in front of setting suns above the sea as big as blazing balloons; rather, it is more about the gift of time to stop and notice and sense the connecting threads, barely visible to the rushing eye, like tearing through spider webs in the early-dark mornings, until some startling frost or dew drops makes them visible.

What was it about reading that God can create everything out of nothing and a new beginning for the sinner (cf. *Catechism of the Catholic Church*, 298) that, at forty, changed my life and made it possible for me to marry? There were plenty of times that I experienced a visit, as it were, of the Lord but none of them were like this passing through the locked doors in the locked room; and, after it, I was able to abandon the misery of every kind of uncertainty and marry. Twenty-three years and eight children later, with three more in heaven, I am able to see that the Lord does not give up; and, therefore, my vocation to love like Him is not to give up either! Thus the graced experience of the liturgical life-cycle of dying and rising entails a turning outwards, ever more widely, as the swathe of problems swell, showing us more and more the common plight of us all or the particularly tragic circumstances of others that need trumpeting above the general noise of deceptively bright busyness.

Finally, I have decided to include a "Guest Poet and Poem" at the end of each section; and, in this way, to enrich the book, possibly widen its audience and too see where it leads; moreover, as in the previous work, *The Prayerful Kiss*, there are plenty of places for the reader to make his or her own notes in the course of reading; but, as you can see, there are some final changes in the title to which I will turn in the Epilogue.

PART I: BEFORE

Beginnings, an ultimate beginning or multiverse imaginings, is there really an in between? Either we think in terms of an endlessness to all that exists, stretching into the past or into an equivalent "imaginariness" as into a pit of practical nothingness, in which beginnings have no beginning and there is the possibility, therefore, that if there is no beginning then there is nothing in existence – which is clearly contradicted by the fact of the universe! For even if it is claimed that the universe does not exist – the claim expresses the existence of it! Or, somehow, there is what exists in a kind of continuously being kept in an everlasting existence kind of state, from everlasting to everlasting, as if there is no possibility of explaining existence beyond the account that it is "there" and that, according to Aristotle, it is kept in a process of change by a First Mover; but, at the same time, this does not explain the very existence of what exists, as if the very idea of a continuously existing universe expresses the possibility of an impossibility of a Being which could bring what does not exist into existence.

In one sense, then, positing what exists and a "First Mover" is almost a natural philosophical account of the state of reality based on what it is like to be a human being; for example, the universe exists prior to us but, being agents of change, we are constantly acting upon it, as it were, and bringing about changes in it. Thus, in a credible kind of way, Aristotle's account very much mirrors our experience of living-in-the-world. Similarly, his idea that there is "matter" and that there is "form", has a credibility about it in that we often take a material, like clay, and make it into a cup, a statue or other object; and, therefore, when it comes to understanding the existence of the human being there is a tradition of thinking in terms of body-matter and spiritual-form: the form determining there to be an embodied human being: a body that expresses a soul: a soul expressing the life of the body. However useful, though, this concept of "body" and "soul" presents a problem of inadvertently imagining that "body" and "soul" are not integrally one. Therefore one of the great challenges to "re-imagining" the relationship between "body" and "soul" is rediscovering their unity! Indeed, it might almost be called biblical phenomenology to consider man, male and female, in their "wholeness".

The poems, then, in this opening part of the book, are looking at the question of a beginning and, as it were, considering the "whole" of what exists as created, whether it be the universe or each human being; for, whatever the merits of theories which entail partial accounts, related or unrelated to human experience, pondering the mystery of created "wholes" leads to a consideration that there is "One" to whom the whole of creation is indebted.

Nothing

In a way it is a rather startling fact that "nothing" does not exist; rather, that something does exist raises all kinds of questions, as we have already begun to see.

In the poem, "Nothing", there is a kind of bare consideration of this fact of what exists; and, at the same time, there is a kind of radical frustration in the writer when it comes to the challenge of communicating these thoughts. Perhaps the most useful image is that the Creator, like a human craftsman, leaves traces of Himself in the very act of creation; and, therefore, it is not so much as what exists "stand alone" as that it "stands in relationship" to being created: to being given existence in very particular ways.

NOTHING
comes from nothing[1]; but not
everything comes from something.

Therefore what comes from something
brings from what it came
something with which it comes.

A picture comes to exist through all the perceptions,
actions, ideas, materials and progress
of the artist.

A word comes forth from the person through all
the events and emotions of living,
the movements of speech, expression and body language:
all expressing relationship.

---

[1] Parmenides' *Physics*, quoted by Dr. Mary Anne Urlakis, as a part of the General Foreword to *Conception: An Icon of the Beginning* by Francis Etheredge, St. Louis, MO: En Route Books and Media, 2019.

A thought goes forth from the maker
and the maker manufactures an object
and the object manifests
the thought of the maker.

Thought is colorless but colors
shapeless it shapes
making visible
what was invisible.

The thought does not cease to be a thought
but is now expressed in an object.

Thought is a thought of the maker
and the maker is more
than the thought of making.

Therefore the maker is greater
than the thought of what is made.

Just as the shiny, sparkly slime,
traces a trail to the snail
so thought is traced to a thinker:

but if beauty is the work of a maker,
and the maker is greater than beauty;

and if what is good is the work of a maker,

and the maker is greater than what is good;

and if truth is the work of a maker,
and the maker is greater than truth –
then the Maker is God:

A wholly amazing Being:
at once so singular and yet the
perfect origin of all relationships;
creative but constant;
and the epitome of a wholly
life-giving generosity
that reaches to the unreachable
depths of reciprocal
self-giving!

OSMOSIS

Just as it takes time, even if only a little while, for different concentrations in a solution to equalize, so it takes time and, possibly, a much longer time, for a husband and wife to settle down together. This is a different kind of beginning to either that of the whole universe or to that of each one of us; indeed, both inhabiting the universe and the beginning of each of us echo and interact with other. Thus there comes the newness of the mystery of marriage and beginning to be 'one flesh'.

On the one hand it is possible that people are unprepared for the change of becoming married and either implicitly or explicitly live it as a provisional relationship, ready to quit it if it does not "work"; or, alternatively, ready to abandon the hope of happiness if it becomes unmanageable. On the other hand, as the poem "Osmosis" develops what emerges is the nature of the equality; and, as such, equality is not uniformity – rather it is about being "equally different" in the "Presence" of "One" who makes communion possible.

There are times, it is true, when one person lives an unbearable sense of not being understood in marriage and there arises the possibility of forgetting the help that God is already giving and what dominates is the "forgetfulness" of "forgiveness": forgetting the reality of being taken from the loneliness of sin to the communion of reconciliation.

Marriage is a whole and God acts constantly in a way that is as subtly hidden and evident as the slow but progressive movement of graced understanding between us; and, like the slow change brought about by the diffusion of grace through the membranes of life, the word of God diffuses through us and brings about what cannot be brought about without Him, the love that He makes possible in showing us we were the enemy He loves into friends.

Osmosis
is the passing
through a membrane:
the semi-permeable "face"
between two different
concentrations of ingredients
so that they equalize.

What,
in the gift and clasp of love,
passes between
husband and wife?

A word,
and within a word,
a promise
being fulfilled.

An arm on the shoulder,
an arm around the shoulder,
an arm around her, holding, passing a healing
through the melting between two
of the distance between us:

a blending of being,
simple and whole,
permeated as if
by percolating
bubbles of oxygenated
conversation and
the help of its source.

What current of love is induced
between us can show
in the life of a child
or the suffering

that arises out of our
fruitlessness.

Equally,
just as what comes
to exist between us is not
wholly from us so also what
is in solution,
present in our togetherness,
spreads out from the
sacramental beginning
of marriage,

the outward sign of my wife and I,

of Christ loving us
through the Church
we make present
in our union.

What passes through us,
in the prayer of our living,
is the life-sustaining
forgiveness of not forgetting
that without the help of God
I would not even
begin to be here.

Osmosis

is a kind of passing

between us of the lives

we lead, without losing them,

where living is a growing

communion through

the "Presence"

of the mystery

making us one,

ever opening,

to receiving from

the Other

and

giving to

the others.

BEGINNING

What is a fact? It would seem obvious to us now, as it always was to a few who were capable of the speculative science, that the world is round; however, for some time, there was a general controversy about whether it was round or flat. In a certain sense, then, there came a point where what was known to a few capable of understanding it became common knowledge for all. Whether it was more and cheaper travel, maps or the beginnings of aviation, it became clear to all that the world was round. In other words, there was already a fact in existence which it was possible to discover; and, in due course, it was discovered. Therefore, even while disagreements ranged from one possibility to the other, there was the fact awaiting definitive recognition.

There is a current controversy about when the human being begins: Is it at the very beginning or at some subsequent point. In general, there is both evidence and a range of arguments that establish it as the first instant of fertilization; and, if there is twinning, at the first instant of the initial separation of human embryonic cells. Whatever the controversy, however, there is a fact: the fact that if a person did not exist and now does, that that person had a beginning. In other words, whatever the controversy, the number of possibilities or the difficulty of identifying the evidence: the fact you and I exist entails that we had a beginning.

Just, then, as we all know that a seed grows, even if we do not know what exactly it is going to be, we nurture its development and wait. However, given that there is a characteristic period of time within which subtle changes take place until, finally, we begin to see shoot and roots, we know that if it is uprooted that it will not complete its early growth and establish itself for what it is. If it does not grow, then, in that characteristic period of time, then it is clear that it was a dead seed or that the soil conditions were contrary to its flourishing. Likewise, as regards the beginning of human beings, we will not see "who" is there if he or she is uprooted or not allowed to flourish. If, however, there is a problem in the womb lining, then there is either the need of expert help or the possibility of adoption needs to be considered.

The essential point is, however, that given that each one of us exists, our beginning is integral to the fact of our existence; and, while there can be controversies about the theoretical questions that that raises, there cannot be a controversy about the fact of beginning to exist being integral to human existence. Therefore, just as we exist there is a beginning to discover to that existence.

BEGINNING
sparks
from Being,
jumping the "gap" between Existence
and the not-until-now being-begun:

an outward universe shouting,
quietly,
of a hidden life,

materializing through clothing what is within
and from what root of thought it first took a start
is now outwardly expressible
in an immeasurable number of
picture-word imaginings:

like fusion's wealth of energy
blasting out an unimaginable amount of power,
as powerfully present as the burning sun,

yet eclipsed,

and as invisible,

as the act of beginning
what did not exist
is Being's
becoming an individual
in the family of man:

like the very different act of Being's
beginning each of us.

In an arcing echo of the beginning's sparking between Existence
and not-until-now-beginning,
leaps a fluorescing of human life

from the tenderest of touches between the
complementary
poles of husband and wife,

like tinder and spark,
but not dry as death,
more like energizing fleshy matter

responding-in-change to change's coming,
igniting developments across the readied
no-longer-cell
or cellularly changeless,

burning fuel that fuels the growth
expressed in movements within and without
all the while multiplying the morphing outward form

from
look-a-like fruit to face
from bubbling growth to growing bubbly
from a singularly distinct beginning to being singularly distinct
from budding to moving limbs making movement possible
from meaning-sounds to sounding speech,
from intelligence inscribed within to talking through thoughts
about life, love and truth,
from immersion in the depths of beginning to exist
to the relationships through which each one of us
comes to exist.

Neither can a whole come from a part
nor an end without a beginning,
although what began can change at the end
and completely refresh the beginning.

To exist
is not a promise,
a theory,
a possibility –
but a
fact.

Just

as a rock,

a plant,

and a planet

exist,

just

as

you

and

I

began,

just

as a beginning,

a change and a

development

exists

so

it is a fact

that we

exist.

We exist

and,

as we once did not exist,

we had a

Beginning.

GUEST POET AND POEM: RAVI SHANKAR

Pushcart prize winning poet, translator and professor Ravi Shankar has published, edited or has forthcoming over 15 books, including the Muse India award-winning translations of 9th century Tamil poet/saint, Andal, "The Autobiography of a Goddess" (Zubaan/University of Chicago), "The Golden Shovel: New Poems Honoring Gwendolyn Brooks" (University of Arkansas) and "The Many Uses of Mint: New and Selected Poems 1997-2017" (Recent Works Press).

Along with Tina Chang and Nathalie Handal, he co-edited W.W. Norton's "Language for a New Century: Contemporary Poetry from the Middle East, Asia & Beyond" called "a beautiful achievement for world literature" by Nobel Laureate Nadine Gordimer and he founded one of the world's oldest electronic journals of the arts, Drunken Boat.

He has taught and performed around the world and appeared in print, radio and TV in such venues as The New York Times, NPR, BBC and the PBS Newshour. He has won awards from the Corporation of Yaddo, the MacDowell Colony, and most recently, his collaborative chapbook, "A Field Guide to Southern China" written with T.S. Eliot Prize winner George Szirtes, was published in the UK by Eyewear Publishing.

He currently holds an international research fellowship from the University of Sydney and his memoir "Correctional" is forthcoming in 2021 with University of Wisconsin Press.

"The Three Christs"[2]:
An introduction by the author Ravi Shankar

I wrote "The Three Christs" after attending a performance by the virtuoso poet Gjertrud Schnackenberg at the University of Connecticut. Her poems are perhaps the closest contemporary example to a poet like John Donne we have today. She is a master of meter and rhyme, and discourses on subjects that range from Russian poetry to Christian theology. A particular favorite of mine among her many fine verses is "Supernatural Love" in which she writes of her relationship with her father and why she imagines carnations to be the flower of Jesus Christ.

"A distant, plucked, infinitesimal string,
The obligation due to every thing
That's smaller than the universe"

the poem goes and the reader's heart can't help but open rapt at the distilled wisdom such lines contain. But thinking about her work and the different strands of Christian poetry, I, an Indian American poet, raised Hindu but with a more Buddhist proclivity for reflection and meditation, nonetheless have entered into the body of Christ and his gospels live in my heart. And I realized that my vision of the prophet

---

[2] "The Three Christs" first appeared in Deepening Groove, the National Poetry Review Prize winner for 2012. ISBN#978-1935716082:
http://www.amazon.com/Deepening-Groove-Ravi-Shankar/dp/1935716085.

has to do with endurance, the ability to survive the slings and arrows of the world, to preserve a sense of love and awe and mystery and gratitude even while being smitten and spit upon by those who uphold different gods.

Not the electrostatic fizz of the Holy Ghost or the vengeful Old Testament rectitude of God the Father, but this humble man, like us, who preached the gospel of love even in a time of division. We live in such a time now and I think that message is of the paramount importance today, even while I believe that the kinds of judgement and Puritanical punishment that many religious zealots believe in today is the very antithesis of Jesus' message. Love your neighbor even if he is black or trans or gay. Do good even if you feel it's not in your own best interest. Don't deny science, but glimpse how in the analysis of those miracles in the germ of each seed, each touch, we are getting closer to understanding the universe and ourselves. That's what Schnackenberg was saying and that's what I believe, but I think the way of getting there is very different; for me at least spiritual bliss is not found at the gilded dictionary of an Oxford-education don but rather in my dealings with the world.

I dedicated this poem to Doug Anderson, a Connecticut poet and Vietnam veteran and atheist, because we had a spirited discussion about Christianity after the reading and I found myself in the odd place of defending faith, even as I cannot countenance the practice of those who act self-righteously in its name. From that origin and discussion came this poem which reflects my own spiritual and aesthetic practice.

The Three Christs
-for Doug Andersen

Waiting for the Norwegian poet to read
her poems, you delineated the differences
between you and her by pointing to Jesus.

Her version, you said, was radiating outwards,
wave and astral particle, revelatory energy
and blinding light, inherently metaphysical.

Your version, however, was dusty and dog-
tired, having walked too long too far in feet
that ached, in draggled robes, in desperate

need of a hot bath, bread, a goblet of wine,
something to take his mind off those carping
apostles, those omnipresent Roman soldiers.

Sitting here, alone, looking out at the play
of sun and shadow on crenellated ferns,
I'm conjuring a third Christ, neither weary

nor luminous, but one who lives nowhere
save within me, indwelling life illimitable
that I will remain estranged from so long

as I insist on insisting, on putting my own

pleasure, which is all I know deeply or well,
first. A Christ who wears my body's garment.

Raise the stone, there thou shalt find me;
cleave the wood and there I am. Let not
him who seeks cease until he finds. When

he finds, he shall be astonished. Astonished,
he shall reach the Kingdom. Having reached
the Kingdom, he shall (shall he? shall I?) rest.

PART II: AWARENESS

There are so many crises that, cumulatively, would sweep us away; but our help lies in the Lord's advice to St. Catherine of Siena: Make your prayer universal and your action real. In other words, whether it is a problem in the marriage, with the children, at work – include all the married, all parents and children and every kind of situation of work: from every type of slavery to impossible-to-spend wealth; and, whether we meet every kind of problem personally we will nevertheless meet, personally, people with problems.

Whether it is the buying and selling of people, of body parts, of life and death or the in between terrible experiences, scarcely to be imagined but always, as it were, on the periphery of our vision, touched upon in the papers, on the news or in those moments of life-experience nearer to death than death itself – there is an impossible heaping of problems, of what seemed like a corner of rubbish collected by the wind turns out to be swarming in a sea like a disaster waiting to break upon the beaches, entangling us all and mounting and mounting in piles pushing into rooms, around corners, up the streets and even becoming home to our brothers and sisters.

Whether it is the experiments that contradict the gift of life to all, equally and almost guaranteed to none; and, in the hands of those given life so freely, are the lives of others handled so carelessly – so unbelievably careless of the life given to others. Whether it is the wealth of nations expended on arms instead of alms. Whether it is power to control instead of serve? Whether it is the chemically contraceptive pollution of the seas instead of helping the pregnant and unborn? Whether it is stockpiling money instead of using it to help. There is opportunity upon opportunity to act before we cannot act and what we did not do endangers our eternal destiny.

But what if, if we even think there is a God, we blame God for the existence of evil and object that if we were the Creator we would not have created a being capable of evil – especially if we foreknew that that being would be as destructive as the devil? What about the limit God imposed upon Himself in order to create a being that is good – but with the possibility of accepting or rejecting that original goodness? Is the power to create not greater if it is possible that all the evil that created beings choose to do is answered in a way that appeals to created freedom rather than rejecting it?

Events, then, raise questions – not least the question of the existence and help of God. Therefore, contrary to the general structure of this book I am beginning Part II: Awareness – with a poem-prayer-question: "Where is He?"

GUEST POET AND POEM: RUSSELL ROGERS

Born 29:08:1934 in Brighton Sussex. I'm a widower, a retired Estate Agent, a father to three daughters and a grandfather to six grandchildren. I live in Cirencester, Gloucestershire. I think of myself as a quiet individual, but still very outgoing. I count myself lucky to enjoy a close relationship with my family and to have lots of friends. These days a good day for me is a couple of bowls matches, finishing off with tea and social contact. My faith is still important to me, together with the friends who go with it.

"Where is He?":
An introduction by the author Russell Rogers

Described as both a poem and a prayer, it was written in less than five minutes. It's raw, not subjected to any rewriting, my usual style. I present it, as it came, from the heart.

Where is HE?
Sitting in my garden, the sun on my face
It's hard to imagine a lovelier place

The spring flowers are all above the ground
Spreading joy and colour all around

But covid 19 is ravishing the land
Why doesn't the Almighty show His hand?

Why doesn't He show us His love?
Instead of hiding away up above

Come on Lord! We need you now
Stand centre stage and take a bow

We've been brought up on the 'Good News'

But all we are hearing is the virus blues

Although we are doing our best and trying
Millions of humanity is dying
Come on Lord! Give us your help today
Show your power! Drive covid 19 away

A TRILOGY OF CASES

Ideas can dominate a society in ways that it is almost impossible to notice or to resist; and, in some instances, this domination is so formidable it almost looks as if it will last. However, there is a difference between truly organically developing doctrines which, in a living way, are always being sought a new form to incorporate the fresh perception of what has emerged since last it was formulated and what is organic but which is encased in an outmoded and almost un-stretchable fixity and, therefore, becomes a strangulated expression of what it is meant to be as its relationship to growth and to the whole of which it is a part is frustrated.

These realities, it seems, can exist both personally and socially; and, in their characteristics, present both personal and wide ranging political choices which, day by day, incrementally open or close the world to a living participation in the dynamics of culture.

PART I: LOCKED

It is clear from a variety of sources, particularly fiction, the media and politics, that there are ideas that are held uncritically and which constitute, in a sense, a prevailing wind and, at the same time, it is with great difficulty that they are engaged – but, nevertheless, the very challenge of them is good for all; for, in their own way, they bring about a deepening of our understanding of the human person in at least three kind of ways: recognizing the value of the point expressed, uncovering what humanizes the point of view in question and, finally, exploring the reasons for the encapsulation of the mind in a limited account of a phenomenon.

One such idea is materialism, the view that all that exists is matter and, in so far as matter is all that exists, all that exists is explainable in terms of the properties of matter; and, therefore, even the philosophical claim that all that exists is matter is to be explained in terms of the properties of matter. However, while it is true that matter is entailed, as it were, in almost every kind of creature or object which has come to exist, it does not follow that the claim that all that exists is matter is itself material. Even if the claim that all that exists is material is expressed materially, whether in the thoughts of the thinker involving the electro-chemical activity of the brain, the sound of a voice or the writing and typing of words on a page, these are no more the complete account of the claim that all exists is matter than that a message "means" the electronic pulse along a phone cable. Thus if there were no phone cable or satellite signal there would be no phone message; but, given the phone mechanism, the message is different from it and unknown to the device that is transmitting it. In other words, just as the meaning of a message is unknown to the mechanical medium of that message, so meaning transcends the material expression of it. Therefore the evidence of matter bearing meaning is evidence that meaning transcends matter and that matter is not all there is; and, indeed, raises the possibility that not only does matter transmit meaning but also that matter is itself meaningful – if for no other reason than it bears the trace of its Maker.

Being locked into a particular idea, however, or being unlocked from it, are themselves subjects open to investigation beyond the fact that they exist.

LOCKED

ideas cloak the mind,
settling down roots in the reason,
rooting people's clogged up thinking,
running tangled knots through oughts
and bungling criticism to the point
of blunting, blocking and blaming others
for imagining a different account
of the same

but uncovered reality.

Fear reaches up to meet the drilled down dumping
with the weight of emotionalism,
mixing a picture out of ingredients
that do not belong together,
making flexibility inflexible
and facts after the image of the mindset,
muddling thinking things through with
being through with thinking.

Clamping down,
pushing up:

the diver surfacing for air holds down the escape hatch;

claws gripping heads into grabbing crabs,

displacing the difference between people
owing to a contagious conformism
crushing observable discrepancies.

Rigidity,
being its weakness,
brittleness being its expression,
blindness being its inoperable effect
and disconnect being the polar
consequence that pushes people
apart in the very meshing
that mats the social mess
into a muted misery.

Witness
the crack that
shells the staggering
secret of its own unworkability
and risks the life of the
seeker seeking the truth.

Who knows who will choose
freedom fulfilled in the truth
over fear inhabited falsehoods?
Are we
locked and limited
or unlocked
and
unlimited?

Are there keys to free
reason for truth
and truth for the reception
of the Word of God?

The Lord limits Himself
to choosing us to be
self-creating creatures of choice
instead of being cast
into an irrevocable mould
of being unable to invoke
His limitless help.

PART II: NAKED

I am thinking of this theme because of reading Viktor E. Frankl's book, *Man's Search for Meaning: The classic tribute to hope from the Holocaust*, in which there is not only his own extraordinarily and beautifully simple account of his life in a concentration camp but there is, within it, a brief dialogue between Viktor himself and a woman, whose name we do not know. The woman is young and is dying and he is, however briefly, her doctor; she says to him:

"'In my former life I was spoiled and did not take spiritual accomplishments seriously" .... "I often talk to this tree", she said to me. I was startled and didn't quite know how to take her words. Was she delirious? Did she have occasional hallucinations? Anxiously I asked her if the tree replied. "Yes." What did it say to her? She answered, "It said to me, 'I am here – I am here – I am life, eternal life'"'[1].

There are many extreme moments, then, some of which we hope either never occur or recur for anybody or, in our fearfully dreadful imaginations, we encounter possibilities that run the risk of unloosening a reaction beyond what is actually happening and committing us, in a way, to taking them for real and really making them so in our unreasonableness. There are images that we retain from pictures taken after the explosion of an atomic bomb towards the end of the Second World War or, equivalently shocking to a young adult's sensibility, seeing the filmed opening of the gates of a concentration camp and the staggering of the bright, wide-eyed, almost smiling men as they came through them.

Thus there are experiences which reveal us to be naked human beings, both literally and stripped of human resources and, while the drama of these times may well vary enormously, one such moment was over forty years ago. I was committed to a locked psychiatric ward,

---

[1] Published in 2004 by Rider, an imprint of Ebury Publishing.

having put the keys through the letterbox of my student digs and set off, not knowing where I was going, but utterly distraught with the impossibility of answering the problem that my life had become: resigning from university, unable to explain to anyone the appalling angst that had arisen in me, friendless, far from home and totally defeated in terms of the objective of knowing what to do with my life – I set off without knowing where I was going and ended up being detained and hospitalized.

In general there are different approaches to mental health and an undue emphasis on drug therapies does not necessarily address the reality of what is going on in a person's life. Even if, then, we sometimes subject ourselves to unusual experiences in the process, there can be a time when our life is almost pinched to the point of brokenness – but crookedly pointing towards a need to answer certain questions.

NAKED

I stood alone
among others on a
locked psychiatric ward.

Exhausted,
- but not delirious -
by the search for meaning;
detained,
incomprehensible to others,
either staff or fellow patients,
I stood alone, naked, to protest

my presence of mind.
What
medicine
could be an antidote
to the metaphysical pain
of the problem of meaning,
meaning the finding of purpose
in failure, after failure,
to prevent the repetition of
repeatedly failing
to find the purpose
of life.

Standing alone,
embarrassed beyond bearing
the sense of the ridiculous
contradiction between reasonableness
and nakedness,
I dressed.

In the mental company
of dissidents,
I learnt their methods
and took and spat the medicine
down the toilet.

Eating, sleeping and working,

-a wrecked student identity scarcely salvageable –
recovers the ordinary routine of life
lost in the weary days of struggling
to get up and get on with a life
whose thread is thinning.

But a framework is not a flower;
A word is not wholly defined by its meaning;
And health is not wholly in the body.

What is a picture-frame without a portrait?
What is an engine without power?
What is a life without purpose?

What is interior needs to be fertilized by what is real[2].
What is interior unfolds exteriorly.
What is exteriorly unfolded expresses relationships:
to the origin of created existence;
to parents and other myriad influencers;
to the actual lived history which flows
through our lives.

Time traps us in a repetition
of unrepeatably different
dead ends –

---

[2] Cf. G. K. Chesterton, *St. Thomas Aquinas*, New York, Mineola: Dover Publications, Inc (from an original published in 1933).

But we discover

after the help

we have received from

the word of God

how indispensable it is

to both understand

and cycle forward!

PART III: RAT-TO-BIRD

There are the hidden moments when, thinking of the railway tracks that others have fallen into, the temptation arises when there seems no relief to the sense of being trapped and hunted out of work by a manipulative employer, playing the legal game and evading responsibility for shifting the terms of work until, finally, all free advice, whether from a lawyer, an employment counselor or others, whether unreachable superiors, or almost all colleagues are found to be unsupportive or, discovering the preoccupation with what is happening at work is detracting from family life – the interminable nature of dead ends all point, finally, to a resignation which turns out to be a liberation to write.

There are other kinds of situations where, as a temporary worker, going to one person as a part of the daily work is like having to squeeze through a slightly barbed gate whereas going to another is almost friendship in terms of the ordinary helpfulness of the person. But there are the more terrible types of imprisonment where the dignity of the person is assaulted in ways too wretched to describe and the person who flays the humanity of another enters, by degrees, more irrevocably into the vice which impales the possibility of renouncing what they have done to the point that, in the end, there needs to be a miracle of healing before heaven is even a remote possibility for them.

There are many kinds of moments, then, whether longer or shorter, which show us our human insufficiency and an answer emerges beyond our capacity and because of prayer.

RAT-TO-BIRD
was first a change from nobody

to admitting administration admitted

me to work
unfolding opportunities,

near and far,
small and significant,
literary, organizational and speaking,

entailing the furthering of education,
experience,
and a structure of work
beneficial to the needs
of a growing family.

But owing to an operation
I returned to discover changes in the structure
amounting to climate change,

growing straight-jacket-strappings
through many small changes changing,

visibly redefining,

each position
to the point of eviscerating
the life-giving gift it once was and,
little by little,
plotting a path of unfulfilling work,
cancelled meetings, interrupted lectures,
early meetings and problematic emails

until

timeless hours turned into tormented times
and the doors I knocked upon did not open

and,

justice unobtainable,
delayed, obstructed and inaccessibly
encased in protocol and processes,
whether witnessed or not ...

When
the way forward

is like going back,
but comes after having been promoted,
it takes a gift of grace to see
that taking flight
is furthering the future
formed through being admitted
to the role of oversight –

turning running away
into a retrospective runway
to an unprecedented horizon
of publishing opportunities!

SHARING

In view of the many times it is possible to pass through a town centre and, even though there are lots of people, we may not recognize anyone and we may not want to, anyway, because of the pressure of a deadline: a date and time when we are hoping to be home, to finish a project or to go out; indeed, this may also apply when we are in Church: that there is always a reason to get away as quickly as we can, with a minimum of delay, to get to dinner, to get through the evening and to get to bed. It is possible to live an anonymous life amongst anonymous people; and, therefore, to be just as unknown as we are ignorant of the lives of others.

But then there is the possibility that in one way or another a change comes over us and, where once we were hurrying by, we pause as we pass and gradually pause a bit longer until one day we actually stop for a while. Outwardly, it could well be that we were influenced by Pope Francis who said stop and speak when we would have otherwise hurried on; but, inwardly, there is that word of God which says "love your neighbour".

This was originally called "Sitting"; however, following my last conversation with Chris, to whom this next poem owes a debt, it is better titled, "Sharing".

SHARING

Sitting

Hatted, bearded, legless, wheel-chaired, selling papers

at first passing, even avoiding,

then perhaps just a glance,

pausing,

then ever so slowly

stopping to talk

but then there are sudden,

unexplained absences.

Now un-hospitalized –

the reasons flow:

Flung upwards,

not flying, but falling

leg lost in a flashing moment

and another,

almost severed,

blood lost,
pain from the pain killer
flown home;

Lost the second leg long after,
too damaged to save,
shrapnel too dangerous to remove,
moving,
painful, at times,
untreatably present
hidden behind pain-stoppers.

We share histories
standing and sitting
as peopled-passing
is interrupted by gifts of
smiling, eats, drinks, a few more times talking; and,
in the glimpsing of many lives lies
the slight crack letting prayers in.

But now the cold has gone below
glovelessly riding a bicycle
in the wintry-Autumn mornings
and has dropped below bearably
clothed-street-sitting in jumpers,
hat and gloves and hot drink and sandwich warm

colding the spot outside the café,

being colder and emptier,
where once he was sitting

but then there are sudden,
subsequently to be explained absences.

Speaking has shared experiences
and who was before unknown is now
known as Chris.

Others come and go on the street,
on sleeping bags, in heaps of cluttered clothes, on cardboard,
on a mattress, in a tent,
alone, together, or in a small group of three,
young and old, clean shaven or weathered

Chris buses regularly to work
to earn the help he needs
to warm through this winter.

Another man has hidden in the bushes,
camouflaged fright,
wounded in his life
unable to live beyond the experience
of memories,
like depth charges,
constantly
witnessing his dying friends,

crying out "Why?" to God
and runs beyond the comfort of knowing
"God loves you as you are".

Another man
plays a piano in the street
so beautifully it is shown world-wide winging help
to begin again a life
hidden, not lost, on the piano-less streets for many years
-      now glowing because of the many gifts amassing fuel
to blow the embers
of a life living
into light.

Chris and I have different lives defined by the
difference between the empty space opened by the death of a dog
and the busy,
peopled passing through people's lives on the street,

and the coming and going in the midst of a growing family

– but he no more knew me than I knew him
and now he calls me "brother" –

but then there are sudden,
subsequently to be explained absences; and I,
and more than I and indeed many more,
wonder where he is on the days of sudden

emptiness where Chris normally sits
to share the lives in passing of
many, many passers-by.

And now we have a common prayer:
for each other; the people passing on the street;
and the past that plagues the present:
the life-long price of war:

Oh pitiless pain
that turns a hand against the heart
that pumps the blood through it!

I beg you, Father, remember
the hidden wounds hurt
and heal them!

I beg you, Lord, let his angel
lead him through the
tunnelling dark!

I beg you, Lord of life,
to let the light of living
dawn again!

FLOWERS

What in the drab dress of winter can pass as garden rubbish is, if considered more carefully, full of life and, literally, budding changes; and, therefore, there is a kind of abundant blindness around us: that we can pass through people's lives without hearing their fullness of years and experience. Thus neglect is almost a "not-noticing" because, perhaps, time is too short to stop and ponder and the deadline, today, is driving us through the breaks into all the time left until it is too late to pause and still we are driven on. There is, then, a tendency to discover the elderly dead because maybe neighbors are too busy to notice, their children are away or there is a growing culture of isolation.

We already know that in a number of countries the elderly are being killed, dying in their homes, withering from loneliness, crawling to an out of reach relative, friend or fellow human being before faltering and failing in health and appetite. We know, too, that there are those who would panic us about sharing what we have; and, instead of realizing how far below is the poverty line, we are made to feel as if we are on a tightrope, wobbly and ready to drop if we give the slightest help to others.

What, in the mix of life, is better than the mixing of the old and the young?

FLOWERS
turned to falling
leaving few amidst the stalks'
timely season's drying in the dying,
withering brightnesses paling into spiky straws,
but drab, well bitten, brittling and rust-spotted leaves
belie the cupped abundance of the brimming seeds:

shooting, even, their slender starts to life
as they sit cupped in open saucers ready
to be dribbled into the earth.

We think that without traction
driving friction
sparking reconciliation,
there will be no development;

but,

alternatively,

seeds already started
slip into the open earth
and in the quiet moist ground
seek out the goodness coming in the damp,
already lying there,
left from many times
rotting down what was good to eat
or life-less, green to brown and fraying,
ready to yield to the cycle
of growing and dying.

But what of the cutting swathes of
unscrupulous grabbing,
targeted stealing,
merciless reaping of body parts,

violations and sweeping exterminations
by those alive to other plans
than that of being brothers and sisters?

Sharing leftovers between us
we understand more
than the careless will ever grasp:
that there is a leap of the imagination,
almost unimaginably wide,
between the ground-broken poorest of the poor
and those whose waste on the plate is
another meal tipped into the bin.

Who will help the burgeoning abundance to be spread
prolifically, prodigiously, even poignantly
to the picked on poor,
targeted as if toxic waste
on a privatized planet
planned to be un-peopled
by all but the aggressively
progressive who?

Seeds once sown
are invisibly active,
then actively visible,
barely above soil,
slender, pale, seeking light,
coloring as they grow and

growing as they color,
brightening and branching out
thrilling through many small changes

so are the slightly bright lovely actions
springing to lighten the long-shadowed days
of the growing old in the companionship of others
where stumbling is an excuse to help,
mumbling almost music-making,
shivering an invitation to eat together.

Sharing is a sliver of goodness so inconspicuously small
in comparison to the wealth of hoarding and yet,
like grain ground to bread could rise and rise again
to spread a sharing like the fall of rain,
on many more and more than many
than started from such poor
beginnings

building an inheritance
out of steps which reach widely
and open on an unmatched horizon
to which, tenderly, tenderness
takes both the tender
and the taken.

THE PICTURE

There is a challenge in describing a familiar situation in an unfamiliar way; and, indeed, what is familiar is no indication of what is just, right or good. In other words we can be so inured to what is actually happening that unless we stood next to it we would not admit its horrific actuality.

This piece, then, is about that dislocation between our own existence and that of others, between the bit by bit reality of human destruction and the difficulty of communicating it, between the noise made to hide the sounds, already almost inaudible and between the widespread number of people already implicated and the intensely personal nature of what is happening.

THE PICTURE
She
drew,
line by line,
pencil pressed,
etched in black,
gripping, painfully, slowly,
smudging her
dripping tears
into the drawing

and tearing,
piece from piece,
the picture

of a child.

Beginning again
she began to draw
and drew again
what she had drawn.

What cycle of grief
will continue
until forgiveness
frees her fingers
from fatal repetition
and returns
her to the run of life?

What gentle grace
will unfurl the fingers
from the grip
of grief?

VULNERABLE

Who is there who has not experienced, directly or indirectly, one of life's innumerable sufferings? At whatever stage of life, in whatever situation, whether through disasters, wars or other ravages of violence, there are events or their scars awaiting redress, explanation or help. Whether we are at fault or another, whether now it was us, before it was others and who knows who it will be in the future, there is always going to be a moment in which we are vulnerable to questioning the purpose of life, the existence of pain, the loss of joy, the want of money and the many, many, many difficulties of being a parent, a relative or a friend or a witness to the reality of life.

Whether our money is so vast, enough or even scarce it does not buy invulnerability – no matter how solid the car, high the wall, electric the fence; we still age, suffer injuries, loss – notice whether or not there is time to talk, to be understood or to find out what we are going through. In other words, the very nature of living entails the death of those close to us; and, if we can but see, of many more around us; and, perhaps, the death of a person close to us opens up a wound through which to see the plight of others.

VULNERABLE

On
waking:
I do not want
to wake up,
get up or go on
facing into the wind.

My anchor is wrenched,
pulled, torn, uprooted
from the bed; and lies
like an ill-fitting key
in the relationships
which remain.

Grief is like a gash,
an unnatural violence
in the flesh of relationships,
not just parting but tearing away
what belonged to be present:
the presence of
a person.

The storm which raged, turned what belonged
in the seabed against itself and,

like the rising of teeth from gums,
the falling of fingernails from hands,
the questioner questioning the very
existence of death,

I am from
the soil which nourished
and grew the pain
which parted
what formed me.

Who are you that send the ruptures
and disclose the weakness,
too trembling, too troublingly complex
and too deep and uncovering
for me to hide in company?

What will catch
the skidding ship
and root again
the trailing
ends of the heart?

Will a fissure appear
between worlds,
slipping a cracking,
to catch the skating
anchor?
Or will a prayer
appeal in ways
trodden by the path
of peoples and seed
a stop to sliding
and pull taught the chain
that chains us to
generations of generous
gifts of grace?

Or will I subside,
like a life submerged,
splutteringly at first
but then quietly
down?

NEWS

There was a time when, growing up, news was as distant and unknown as the planets or the far flung places in the universe; existing, all the same, but beyond the possibility of being seen by someone who was not looking. As a child who only saw the streets, the people at home or over the road, or the garden in which we jumped over the roses and dug holes in the ground beneath the tree beyond the grass; indeed, how fortunate I was, in a way, to be able to be fascinated by my first pair of spectacles – Noticing, as I walked, how much clearer everything was!

Now, almost anyone or anything brings news, whether it is the children from their day, the papers, the internet, the radio or even a noticeboard; indeed, news is everywhere coming in, whether in articles to be read, books to be studied or courses to be attended. Taking, then, the word 'News' as suggesting what, literally, is new, it is almost impossible not to go through the day on a kind of running influx, input or background swell of what is going on here, there or practically anywhere in the world.

NEWS

comes after the silence,
even stillness,
of the children leaving for school
and, working from home,
although not alone,
there are small chores to
warm up on and flex

the cold legs.

In the middle of the morning,
a cup of coffee and tea, too,
a biscuit and taking the rubbish out,
where twigs and plastic bottles
are scattered by the storm.

Elsewhere
the trees are blown down
and roads blocked,
traffic diverted, cars overturned,
fences broken,
and power lost.

News can drive,
driving devastation into peace,
whether it is the risk of our children
being set upon after school,
the possibility of accidents,
injuries or the wider worries
of illness, untimely deaths
or abduction.

News
breaks of atrocities,
past and present and, for some, ongoing
in an unspeakable way.

Would it really be better not to know?

Would it really be safer for our children?

As if amidst the debris from a wrecked ship,
turning up on the shore,
peoples' lives are scattered
on the waters,

wondering
if anyone will see,
if anyone will get wet,
if anyone will help.

What of the turmoil within,
the questions and silence
of those who do not return?

Imagination populates the scarcely reported
scarring tragedies in the lives
of so many living people.

There is no longer the silence on the street
or the button on the media;
there are no more walls to people's
sufferings.

The intimations of the reality of people's lives
grow, with experience,
into the detail out of which
prayer emerges.

What of the days of struggle
and uncertainty about tomorrow?

What of the everyday problems
that mount an attack
on our peace?

Does not good news arise
like the survivor out of the storm,
sodden but unrepeatably there,
not disregarding or ignoring
those who were lost,
but a blessing that yet turns us
to blessing God.

Is it not better to pray
and to persevere
in what we do
rather than to
despair and die?

To help
in a small way

is better than

not doing a

great work.

A Trilogy of Tones: Black; White; and Grey

If we want a voice to stand out from the crowd we have to listen to a particular person; and, if we want a crowd to become a group of people, then we have to listen to each one of them; and, if we want a group of people to become known to us then we have to get to know them.

Calling all "cultures", "religious denominations", "world faiths", philosophers and indeed anyone of good will, as I am thinking of a trilogy of poems called "Black", "White" and "Grey". This was inspired by seeing a collection of large photographs at a local exhibition, showcasing the variety of peoples that lived in a city. What do you think are the colors of your culture? What strengths and weaknesses? What bright spots and challenges?

It is also true that "Black", "White" and "Grey" are stereotypical tones. In reality, as with all lives, each individual life is both immersed in a place, a culture and the many aspects of society to which he or she is connected, either temporarily or more enduringly; and, at the same time, each one of us is iridescent with the very individuality and relationships through which we live, express ourselves and from whom we receive so much and to whom we are called to give so much. On the one hand these pieces of prose and poetry are about the challenge of thinking differently about words and that to which they refer; but also, on the other hand these poems, with whatever limitations they possess, are about calling into question those stereotypes and celebrating the impossibility of doing justice to real people[3].

BLACK

This first piece proved more difficult to write in that I did not want to write about specific people, although specific people prompted this trilogy; and, I confess, I did not read all the biographies of those photographed – but enough to realize that there is no uniform black experience any more than there is a uniform "black person".

It was, then, while pondering the problem of how to write these pieces, or abandon this trilogy, that I sent a text to one of my daughters saying that I was struggling; and, she replied, as the weather is good, to go outside with my notebook. The day, however, as bright as it was cold and, being both tired and cold, I did not relish sitting outside; nevertheless, I did go out into the garden and thus I began to notice how many different kinds of black there were; and, as you will see, I began to think about "black" and write, in a way, of my experience of it.

Thus, in a rather unexpected way, began the writing of this first piece called "Black". Perhaps, in an equally unexpected way, black turns out to be very present in all kinds of ways and, almost, has a kind of durability about it in that it can bear the wear and tear of weather

---

[3] This is adapted from a post on LinkedIn, the business website on which I advertise my work, in that people read my work across the world; and, therefore, responses have both enriched these pieces of prose and poetry but, also, this served as a thank you to all those who read what I write.

more easily.

BLACK
is an abstraction: a concept in the imagination:
informed but textureless and shapeless –
related to what is sensed but poor
by comparison with the real.

The question is: What is black?

Stereotypes are words stuck in unthinkableness.

Black history; black people; tribal; decorated dancers; slaves; athletes;
models; actors; doctors; nurses; politicians; activists; jazz musicians
and soul singers.

But to the person who looks,
black is as varied as actual black objects.

Black soil, damp, broken eggshells break the surface, small stones,
moss a speckled greenness, flattish, leafy outbursts, pooled water
glassy-black-bright and replete with changing reflections; and,
as it happens, black compost, browny tinge, bringing out the
best of the earth and its plants.

Green bushy Ivy, clumpy, not like clay, gathering round the tree
trunk and deep greeny-dark shadows dying into black but still green;
and black tulips, cupped and colored, velvety, almost hairy,

stood upon green stems too various, like black, too describe.

Sky, star-bright speckling, deeper than the deepest sea,
depths unimaginable, colored gases too distant to see,
darker than the light-less places are the deepest black-holes –
stopping even the light being emitted from a collapsed star:
gateway to perplexing
physics and phenomenal strangeness
to our everyday experience of gravity.

Black bears, huge, teethy, and black panthers, lithe and slinky;
black patches in many creatures, big or small, whether cows
or cats, quick or slow and, on examination, mixed up
with many colors.

Driving in the dark evenings, wet and cloudy times, rain on the
windscreen, puddles on the roads, cyclists almost invisible
in their colorless clothes, relying on being seen in poor visibility
as if being reluctantly visible is more important than being seeable.

Black shoes, laced, unlaced, buckled, Velcro, shiny, matt,
etched and patterned, polishable or permanently shiny black;
and black suits, smart, tailored to fit, whether for weddings or
funerals, formal or fashionable, expensive or less.

Black biros, ink, lids and pen ends, black liners
that make the drawings stand out, emphasizing the
main lines of the drawing, framing the shape and stylish

movements of the draughtsman.

Black bin-liner semi-filled, crumpled, shiny, shadowed, black or empty, flat, wet and lying across the ground – or given arm holes and worn as a raincoat on a pilgrimage.

Black road, smooth and patchy, as if pebbled, gritty and blacker wet.

Black computer box, shiny front reflecting wires and the room, matt sides, slotted, technologically bright, buzzing, wired and blacker shadows.

Black is everywhere, a part of everything, naturally, deliberately, and by design.

WHITE

Ice and snow landscapes lie, like a landslide, on the imagination; and, in their dramatic apparel, shape the first thoughts of white and, in a way, need shaking off and thinking through more thoroughly. There were curling turns of snow, wrapping up and around hedges in the less well traveled roads of the villages in the North of England; or, in long exposure photographs, an almost burnt intensity to the detailed lines and patterns of slowly studied scenes of snowy scapes. As regards my childhood, I can remember sliding on whitish roads which then grew brown and slushy and, even more recently coating, thickly, even the washing lines and edges of fences and objects – but then, like the origin of writing marks, the marks of padded feet pass across the whites we witness and, little by little, the colder grey of snowy-ice appears.

White, like black, is an oversimplification; however, thinking it through raises thoughts of vulnerability: of a surface too bright to hide the marks and strokes of the weather, like the road dirt that clings to the once almost white car after a few long journeys.

WHITE
Having begun with black
white is also a stereotype: a fixed idea:
an idea set in type as if it is a singly repetitive thought:

ruler; rich; male; civilizer; racist; exploiter; explorer; scientist; writer;
sailor; soldier; inventor, merchant and musician.

What is white?

White, unbroken light, seen across the cloud mountains, ranging,
rising in colossal lumps and clumps, but level,
as when the plane flies above a fluffy rock field
below the bluey sky-scape, stunningly bright, like snow,
and even ice-bright, blindingly brilliant, splashing everywhere.

White are the sparkles, the sea-star-studded spots of brightnesses,
as if the sky is earthed and the stars are loosed upon the waters,
or scattered everywhere in the twinkling of dew-drops
of a sunny morning, before the evaporation, atop each blade of grass
– as if a glass blower had bubbled over every standing tip

and tipped it with a stunning bauble.

White are the outbreaking stars sieved, as it were, through the
immensity of space, breaking through the beautiful background
as if the starting of plants or the budding of seed potatoes,
an impression of immensely sprouting energies
blooming through the porous night sky.

Polar bears, just visible, like the arctic fox, finding their food
in places surprising and, for all their beauty,
almost barren.

Bride white dresses, intricate or plain, with or without hats and veils;
but, being white, like school shirts,
show the grime and broken pen's ink smatterings,
scarcely washable and worn once in the hope of a
once-for-all wedding gift of bride and groom.

White paper, readied for drawing and painting, accommodating
almost any design and colour scheme, shape or pattern
but, once marked, marks remain.

"Whites": once new fridge; freezer; fridge-freezer; sinks; baths; tiles;
toilets, with or without seats; cupboards and cars;
shiny, scratched, slightly rusted, holed and stained.

White is scattered, present and occasionally prevailing;
but, often, benefits from color and contrasts.
Black and white need each other!

GREY

What has this accomplished? This trilogy of "Black", "White" and "Grey". It has certainly forced me to think in terms of what, in existence, expresses these tones; and, perhaps, to think of looking at ordinary things in an unusual way, given that it is difficult if not impossible to generalize about the cultural reality which each one bears within. There are examples in every culture of the great successes, of overcoming adversity, and indeed there are the tragic failures of being overcome. At the same time "Grey" could have stood for the indeterminate, vague, neither one thing nor another, neither great success nor terrible failure, but instead turns out to be a transitional tone – signifying that the author, artist, sculptor, musician and human being is always "between" states of one kind or another and is never, not in this life anyway, a finished, fired pot.

Perhaps entering eternity is like being "fired", as with a permanent glaze, as if dropping out of temporality is like dropping into the true permanence of who I am: Of what degree of love registers as my final expression of the fruit of being loved!

GREY

is an in between tone:
between black and white
and ranging throughout the colors,
as when the light recedes and the shadows strengthen
and the brightness mutes before
becoming darker if not dark as black
or, conversely, the grey glows light-bright-white.

Grey skies are anything but dreary grey
but it takes time and patience to see the obvious,
cold, chilly beauty in the colder silvery colors.

Grey could be nondescript: a fading or discoloring
of true colors, evocative of "indifferent days",

alternatively grey could
be a traveling color,
transitioning between the different
destinations of light and dark,
each equally different but both equally good.

Would time travel be grey?

Zooming through tubeless wastes,
rotating, twisting, twirling at imaginary speeds,
doing untold damage to the history of the travelers,
zipping them out of existence or into existentially
ancient states of health
and a truly horizontal longevity that might
dramatically change.

Grey
is the symbol of gradations:
the always in a state of change reality of us all;
color could be described as the moment
of an accomplishment: the beauty of a destination:

the time of a display.

Dying
could be described as slipping out of the greys
that characterize change and manifesting,
once and for all,
the color of love.

AWAKENING

There are, as we know, many starting points to writing. This one was as a result of reading John O'Brien's, *A Love Supreme*, where he said: "The trials and pains of the world can silence this voice for a while. We are never far from the grace of God. He continues to reach out to touch us. We have to become sensitive again to his voice"[4].

On the one hand, it is true, there is a hardening of which the psalmist speaks when he says, "Do not harden your hearts as at Meribah" (Ps 95: 8), as when the people complained in the desert that God, who took them out of Egypt, was not able to provide water for them in the desert; and, indeed, we can complain about our limited income, weak health, the faults of wife and children, the drawbacks to where we live – and indeed about almost everything! If this complaining, when I hear it from the children, drains enthusiasm, discourages and fills me with bitterness – What is the effect on God

---

[4] From an original text supplied by the author, John O'Brien, Frater, OFM (Franciscan), p. 53, otherwise published under the same title on Amazon: https://www.amazon.co.uk/Love-Supreme-John-OBrien-OFM/dp/1687860106.

who provides all we need? Is it that we need the sting of the serpent (cf. Num 21: 4-9) to wake up to the gratuitousness of what we are given?

On the other hand, the word of God "does not return to me empty, without carrying out my will and succeeding in what it was sent to do" (Is 55: 11). The land, then, is dependent on the rain to nourish what is in it and so are we dependent on the word of God to be sent to us so that it will succeed "in what it was sent to do". In other words, what makes us sensitive to the work which makes the soil receptive to what is sown? Just as the ground cannot prepare, plant and water itself, so there is a radical dependence on God sending a word which accomplishes what it was sent to do. That radical dependence is a fruitful poverty; and, therefore, whatever helps us to see and accept the neediness that makes us beggars before the Lord hopefully helps us to beg the sensitivity we need to make His word seed.

AWAKENING
is sudden, unpredictable, wondrous:

hoped for – but unexpected!

the pale, swan necked, uncurling,
starting, startlingly, stirring,
seed-breaking the soil –

surprising us!

Wearing the skin of the seedcase it arises,

nightcap crowned,
growing taller, passing through
fledgling-dragon-wings,
increasingly willowy,
stem talling,
leaves like opening ears,
having heard the call of growth
the first solar panels
accelerate the soaring up!
What inaudible call
welled from without
the mystery of moisture
opening within the
reaching into the light?

What
word unfolds
the deepest being,
hidden, soil deep, awaiting
a stir from within
the inert life into a swirling swelling
expansion of structured
greening?

What
taking up
from dead soil
turns subtle traces of essential elements

into multiplying
cells increasing the outer size
and amazing the gardener
with the speed and surefooted
stepping-stairs
to maturity?

We
are familiar
with a word within
breaking into speech,
sentences, books, scripts
conversations –

Yet
there is
a mystery to the
working within
through which
we live
mirroring
the word which passes
through to plant
eternal life.

GUEST POET AND POEM: FR. ANTOINE ALTIERI

I am 47 years old and a *docteur de la faculté de philosophie de l'Institut Catholique de Toulouse* and a *Directeur d'études*. My philosophical studies are about the relationship between theology and philosophy (especially the philosophy of art).

"LA GRAND SANTÉ (GREAT HEALTH)": An Introduction by the author, Fr. Antoine Altieri

This text is based upon two philosophical insights: as its title suggests, a Nietzschean one (the topic of "Great Health", or that of "eternal return", in which we can be given to live every moment fully), but also the famous verse of Hölderlin: "*Aber wo Gefahr ist, wächst das Rettende auch*" ('But where the danger is there also *grows* the saving power'[5]). The poem intends to evoke some kind of transfiguration of facticity in something that might be like a "grace".

LA GRAND SANTÉ (GREAT HEALTH)

Nous demandons : à quoi se résume une vie ?
Au nombre de nos jours vécus sous le ciel nu ?
A ce que l'on y fait - à ce que l'on oublie ?
Au souffle maintenu,

---

[5] Mr. Martin Higgins, MA: the German expression, literally translated, means: 'But where the danger is there also *grows* the saving power'; or more freely: 'where ever there is danger present - there is also generated the power that can save' (email, 23/03/20).

We ask with bated breath:
how do you measure a life:
By the number of days passed under an empty sky?
By what one has achieved or by what has passed us by?

Identique à soi-même, au-dessus du néant ?
Nous avançons inquiets, esclaves de nos pas,
Moitiés d'aveugles fous, misérables, marchant
Vers l'ignoble trépas.

True only to itself above the void
We tread fearfully, slaves of our chosen path
In half blind madness, miserable, towards a pitiful end.

Cela seul est certain, de tout ce dont on glose,
Et nous allons pourtant notre train chaotique,
Nous réjouissant de peu, de vin ou de musique,
Du rouge d'une rose -

Only this is true, all else is a sham
And yet we continue our chaotic way
Sometimes rejoicing with wine or music
or the red of a rose

Comme si l'Ennemi qui flétrit toute chair,
En de rares instants de paix et de clarté,
Etait soudain lui-même englouti dans l'éclair

De la Grande Santé !

As if in moments of peace and clarity

the enemy which withers all flesh

was suddenly engulfed by a luminance of great well being[6].

---

[6] A "free" translation by John and Charlotte Martin of a French poem by Fr. Antoine Altieri, called: "*La Grand Santé*", 1/04/20 which was approved by Fr. Antoine, 14/4/20. But I would also like to acknowledge the help of Nicole and Barry Griffin, too, who worked on a different translation from the French.

Part III: Technological Leaping

There are great discrepancies in the world between the technological development of one country and that of another and between one place and that of another, besides the fact that one country may be the dumping ground for the electronic waste of another; and, therefore, it is not so much whether a country has been through the whole process of technological change or whether or not it has arrived at a very late stage of development without having been through earlier ones. Rather, it is about the "leaps" and "bounds" that have taken place and will continue to take place throughout the working world. The world has become a "talking shop" and, from every part of the globe people are able to see the wealth, the sophistication or the "want" from wherever they are to wherever it is.

There is, however, amazing progress that has been made, and is still to be made, in the area of computer assisted limbs, machines and communication devices for the physically impaired; and, particularly, for those whose illness steals the least possibility of communicating. Thus it is wonderful to see that a man, in the later stages of motor neurone disease, can communicate by "writing with his eye movements" on a specially adapted keyboard; and, therefore, one imagines the possibility of some general assistance to faulty or failing nerve messages in the future. In other words, in one of the great advances of technological aids, there opens up the possibility of enhancing, if not reversing, those suffering from profound disabilities.

At the same time, however, the question of some kind of "bionic" man has been around for some time; and, little by little, accessories are going beyond the help required by people with extreme communication problems or the need for help with missing, lost or damaged limbs. Thus we seem to be entering a "grey place" between robots and robotic-like-abilities. One fear would be the "armouring", as it were, of the human being. Just as "armour plate" shields a car or other vehicle from dangerous weapons, perhaps armouring the human being will make him or her insensitive to the ordinary touch of human tenderness; and, therefore, just at the point where human beings need to be more sensitive to each other there will be a danger of becoming less so – increasing, then, the likelihood of "bionic" combat.

All in all, will the "technological leaping" take us beyond the humanization of human beings and enter us, like it or not, into an era of living science fiction; or, in fact, will the technological help to those already suffering profound physical or communication difficulties go on being helped, more and more?

SKIN DEEP

In one sense, I am sure, changes have many sources and, perhaps, no one single origin is explanation enough except the creativity with which we are endowed and the extractability of the universe in which we are both immersed and immeasurably made to transcend.

There will always be changes, more easily traceable as the past amasses simplicity as it passes into the present, changes that are always open to a further and fuller explanation, account or leading trail of discovery; indeed, changes in one field of endeavour or expertise stimulates those in another, ever reaching scales, great or small, perhaps once unimaginable or unimaginably slow, like walking to the moon is now walking on the moon and has now extended to sending sensors deeper and deeper into the depths of the universe.

The speed of change may well depend on our proximity to what drives it, whether ingenuity, wealth, technological innovation, labor costs or even the stealing of the cost of labor, mechanization of production, exploitation or use of resources; indeed, just as with the world of culture as a whole, there will be people to whom all is unintelligibly different and almost incomprehensible and there will be those for whom change is too slow and regulated.

Nevertheless, it is not just a matter of what happens it is also a matter of what kind of impact it has; and, therefore, do the changes help to humanize our relationship to one another or do they accentuate differences to the point of making war more possible, deadly and inhuman?

SKIN DEEP

As a child

grown into a man,

so what began with a television screen

coming like a cinema into the sitting room

has grown into a world-wide change

with each child holding

a screen in the hand

or seized by the hope

of being handed one.
As a youth I drove a tractor
in the fields and along the roads
as the harvest was gathered from fields
a little too far to walk with heavy loads

and now my children cross the world
at a glance.

Machines have changed the landscape,
whipping off and beating down the top of the hedge,
or mechanically heavy, cumbersome, lumbering,
powerful earth movers, load bearing, massive diggers,
bridging gaps, building tall and small, on or under the ground
and changing the course of rivers.

Scaling down to domestic uses
still costs industrial wealth.

We can wear devices to become usefully powerful
or monstrously deadly;
they can aid us in our disabilities and disasters
or they trap us into securing our safety:
armoring our cars, houses and places of work;
they can accentuate the difference between us:

Rolls Royce or cart, tank or trolley,
surveillance or feedback

or they can shorten the gap between us
to make sympathetic action possible.

.

Shrinking machines,
not simply smaller and smaller,
once shaping the ground around
are now taking the shape of the body –
once outside the skin are now going under it;
gadgetry of many media-kinds:
smarter; smaller; quicker;
almost instantaneous – crossing the world
with a message, an image, news,
and even shrinking global distances,
undermining our ignorance of other
people's difficulties.

What human price are these changes paid in?
What hours of manufacturing, working conditions and wages
are behind the advancing of skin-deep
technological leaps?

We are captivated,
if not captured in a computer driven web
of interconnecting signals,
almost frozen like a rabbit in head-lamps,
suffering a mild but paralyzing shock,
keeping us connected.

But our wired or even wireless
connectedness is still
slower and more complex than the
heart beaten prayer.

FLITTING

This seems to be an increasingly characteristic activity for anyone working with the social media; indeed, whether working with it or not, it seems to be what happens when people engage with electronic media.

To begin with, it seemed as if it was necessary to have a "social media platform" and a place from which to dive into the internet, advertising work which, while slowly written, seemed to have the possibility of rapidly reaching a wider and wider audience; however, over time, even with the deliberate action of making every click onto a media site a moment to send an advertisement, it does seem as if the payback in terms of book sales is scarcely noticeable. On the other hand to know that a piece of writing has been read in several states of America, several European countries, China, Australia and many others has a kind of compulsive reckoning about it even if, in the end, practically nothing comes of it or there is the occasional exchange of ideas.

More importantly are the people with whom a working relationship has developed and who have become, in the genuine sense of the terms, both collaborators and colleagues; and, at the same time, there are the few who will probably explore what has been actually written and, one day, might write a review of it. Then there are also the "news items" that change, constantly, highlighting a whole variety of work and activity that ranges from innovation to notoriety; and, as such, could end up as a kind of compulsive distraction as one image after another finds justification to be clicked and read.

But does this make the whole use of social media worthwhile; indeed, how do we measure, apart from the hoped for financial return and the cost of lost writing time, the value of what has been done? One very great unknown, apart from the long-term effect of all this advertising, is whether or not a word has been helpful to anyone; and, not just helpful as in an interesting read, although that has its place – but helpful in helping a person turn to God for help. Maybe we will never know, this side of eternity, whether or not a word-in-the-ether has landed on a needy shore and saved them from wasting their lives, stepping under a train or taking a wrong turn.

FLITTING
between screens
is adding
time to time and taking more time.

What drives glimpsing another shot?

To see what was almost seen a second before shooting
another glance again at similar sights
so soon as to be almost simultaneous,
taking more and more time,
from writing and reading
and sending it into an electronic

hole of vastly expanding proportions,

where scrolling down the screen is treading time,

draining time after time of passing between
colorful, interesting images and attractive sounds
and often sound and sage sayings,
many wiser than the reader reading
who, not so subtly, is simply
flitting between screens?

Is it winning?

Is it like watching
on the edge of our seats as a goal
is about to be scored: that hold your breath moment,
or is that it is fun and our friends are doing it
and the pressure builds to participate,
or is it that our hopes and dreams are hooked
into an impression of buzzing-about-to-be-realized
if only, only, only someone will see
the possibility
of winning through some wisdom
in what is written?
Or is it that the very clicking that connects
the process of progressing to an experience of walking:
a one-step-at-a-time pace
of going from nowhere to somewhere –

from anonymity to being anonymous no more:

a virtual success in that one click has met another
and together these clicks tick that box of being noticed
which counts click upon click until the numbers

go up and up and up as if,
like bingo, a bell at the top of a pole or the tipping of a scale -
there is going to be a prize?

Or is flitting a compulsive
twitching between screens:
a kind of kinetic kick from screen to screen?

Flitting
is not without its feedback
in that writers write back and,
if not directly,
reinforce the very words
to which a reply was made.

Finally,
passing up on passers by
who appeared to have no connection with work,
there are those few and far between
who have become friends,
beginning with a few words that hatched a helping
throughout a growing number of years

like the branches of a tree upon which perch

birds and squirrels,

more lively and beautiful

than what grew

from the slightest of beginnings:

the gathering of words!

PHONEHEADS

Maybe the very title of this section betrays an annoyance with what is, almost, an example of a "bionic" technological takeover; as, very often, the use of a phone goes well beyond the sending and receiving of messages.

On the one hand, then, there is a distinct advantage to being able to text a friend or research an interest, never mind make a call in an emergency; and, in many cases, where family are separated or children few, it obviously allows for people to keep in contact with each other. Indeed, one of the oft repeated claims of a book, reviewing Pope Francis' use of twitter, is that "A new papacy was afoot, and though the world didn't yet know it, so was a new way of connecting everyday Catholics to their spiritual leader. The Tweetable Pope was powering up"[1]. There is, too, the amazing reality of being able to receive birthday greetings from the other side of the world, via satellite, on even a simple "brick" phone. But, on the other hand, there are all the disadvantages of unsupervised and unhelpful use of cameras, search

---

[1] Michael J. O'Loughlin, *The #Tweetable Pope: A Spiritual Revolution in 140 Characters,* Oxford: Lion Hudson, 2016, p. 29.

engines and being "on-line"; and, as the title of this piece suggests, "Phoneheads", there is a tendency, as many images show, for the head to be bent over the phone and, whether or not anyone else is around, for the person to be "connected" to "elsewhere".

Thus, as a parent, there is a constant challenge not just to protect and moderate the use of phones but, in general, to encourage a wholesome range of human activities; and, while it is always a challenge, to stimulate the "other" range of doing which is to do with drawing on the talents of the children. Thus, over the holidays from school there is the goal of defining and executing a project, whether bringing a story to completion, designing and mounting a small set of football drawings, a family outing, learning to cook through helping with a meal and, at the same time, taking a turn with housework chores.

PHONEHEADS

The
anatomy
of an object
follows that of
a body.

The whole
human being
communicates within
and with others.

Noise
isolates
the person
by saturating
the senses.

Gadgets
have climbed
onto the head,
into the ear,
and around
the neck.

A phonehead is
one word from two
disparate parts:
head and phone:
one word a symbol
of both the creative
leap and the leading of
technologists.

Wires
drooping down
from around the ears
and phones held
between "using"
and "immersion".

Imagery and sound
sounding imagery
imaging sound:
like a seal surrounding
the senses exclusively
sensing the imaged
sounds.

What if the screen
screens what is
to be seen?

How
is reality to be seen
from behind
a screen or is the mind
to be shrunk to fit it?

When
will release
come to the cloning of heads:
the planting and transplanting of what
has been repeated and repeated
and repeated elsewhere?

What in-breaking of sunlight on the clouds,
what mist softened and partially stolen shapes
of red-eyed wind turbines,

turning through time while generating energy
in as relaxed arcing as cartwheeling across the landscape,
languishing in the watery,
soft-hued awakening of the morning:
sun stripped of burning brightness,
cloudiness soaking up the glow,
leaving a bright impression
of a pale-white disc amidst the day's
breathing, breath-taking mistiness.

What glimpsing of sight
is left in the stealthily
silencing of seeing?

Will addiction dawn
or loss of contact with the splendidly free-range
variations of the changing landscape
spur the release of the pawn
from under the paw of
gadget-giants?

Or will the "phone" grow like a growth,
smothering imagination and conversation with
the plugged in sealing off of the senses and the
surround-sound and bubbling imagery and texting,
swiping, sliding, screen deceiving busyness
of being busy in a swimmingness
of slightly filtered tumbling

media messages.

But

contact is

good, helpful, even

necessary

and essential!

Conversations are now possible

that were never even thought possible;

or, by letter, took months

to take place.

Connections vary:

signals vanish, interference smothers

the connecting radio waves,

batteries fail and phones die.

Untiring wiring:

prayer's passage:

is direct, full and clear

and faster than the

fastest fibre-optic messaging

and calls, ceaselessly,

on the waiting, watching, living

of lively exchanges between

the word of God

and the pulsing inter-activity of

His Church and the world

in the daily life of each

and all of us.

GUEST POET AND POEM: RICHARD DJJ BOWDERY

Richard's passion for "making poems" has, over the years brought him some success. To date he's published four collections of verse and his work has featured in several anthologies. He has also recited his work at spoken-word events in and around London.

Richard was also instrumental in setting up two poetry groups. The first was formed in the 1980's with colleagues from the communications giant BT. And in 2013 he co-founded The Croft Poetry Club in Kent with fellow poet Jerry Dowlen.

Now semi-retired he is using the time to write new poems which will be published on his website:

richardbowderywriter.wordpress.com.

"NOMOPHOBIA NO MORE":
An introduction by the author Richard DJJ Bowdery

Today's technology, computers, tablets, Smart TVs, gaming consoles, mobile phones and such like, have become a key part of everyday life. Most people own one or more of these products.

Today's technological advances come with many benefits: online banking, purchasing, virtual face-to-face communications, information gathering, entertainment to name but a few. But there are downsides as well.

Fraud can be achieved from the comfort of a fraudster's armchair. For example, how many spam emails do you receive daily offering you your wildest dreams?

Then there are governments who can spy on its citizens with

impunity. Our electronic footsteps leave a trail of activity which can be followed by any 'virtual' stalker. Our every move is monitored. Our daily routine written on some database diary somewhere. Little, if anything, is hidden from view.

But of all these negatives chief among them, in my opinion, is technology's ability to isolate us from one another. And of all our devices the worst offender for this is the mobile phone.

In a restaurant, at bus stops, on the bus, on the train, around the dinner table, in the office, on the beach, in the country or at the shops people are drawn to their mobiles like moths to a flame.

And where better to witness this phenomenon than on any street in almost any country across the globe. People walking, head down, spellbound by the object they clasp in one or both hands.

But why do I think this is worse than the other two examples I alluded to — fraud and big brother?

Well we can't stop fraudsters trying to con us. Nor can we halt governments from poking about in our personal electronic journey. We can, however, decide to isolate ourselves.

We have a God-given ability to communicate which isn't replicated in other parts of creation in the same way. We are social creatures. We need to interact with one another. Yet we are allowing technology to blinker us from this. For instance, how many friendly greetings are missed because one passerby has his head stuck in a mobile phone? And how many conversations are lost because, well why talk when you can text?

There are also wider implications for our texting generation. I've been a reader of newspapers for many years. Today I've noticed more spelling and grammatical errors within their pages than ever before. Is this as a result of speed texting where what the sender wants to say is implied and not necessarily spelt correctly or grammatically correct?

My poem seeks to highlight the conundrum we have engineered for ourselves. Some will say it suits me to have this technology with the benefits it affords. I simply ask at what price? As with everything there is a price to pay and it isn't always monetary.

Do we want to shut ourselves off from others? Do we desire to become even more insular than we already are?

Because our brains are so wired we view face to face messages and texts on a phone in completely different ways.

Visual signals when people are face to face confirm the tone of a spoken message. A text doesn't have that luxury and so is open to a myriad of interpretations. We can often pick the wrong one because we can't see what is meant. Emojis can lessen the misunderstanding but not always. No amount of emojis could have saved the person in my poem.

In closing I leave you with this thought. 1918 saw the world plagued by Spanish flu which caused terrible destruction before slithering into the history books. In 2020 Chinese flu spread its tentacles around the globe. It too will, in time, be consigned to history. But self-distancing, a vital defensive tool for the government to help stem the spread of both viruses, will remain. Not because of any deadly disease. But because of how we allow our use of mobile phones to dictate a lack of engagement with our fellow man.

NOMOPHOBIA NO MORE

Head bowed as if in meditation,
Hands cradling this object of desire,
Pupils dilated blur the vision,
Man snared by a digital choir.

The screech of brakes punch through the air,
Metal to flesh has only one outcome,
Bloody hands loosen their tight grip,
New text message — you can't claim asylum.

PART IV: GRACE

The word "grace" is particularly challenging; and, indeed, needs some kind of explanation. On the one hand "grace *escapes our experience* and cannot be known except by faith" (CCC, 2005[1]); and, therefore, is it like reading invisible writing: as if the grace is a word written in lemon juice and needs a flame to show its existence? Perhaps there is truth in this: that "*grace escapes our experience*" if our experience is that we need, in a humanizing way, to recognize that our neediness is what we have in common with others and that, in a way, the common experience of human beings is the discovering, often through adversity, of our neediness and indeed that of others. But grace goes beyond recognizing our neediness even if, in a certain kind of way, it is beginning to guess that there is something on the paper to be read because it smells and looks a bit crumpled. In other words, "*grace escapes our experience*" until an action or word of God, where one is inseparable to the other, passes like an event in our life and leaves us different in a way that we know is beyond us.

Grace is the action of God. Thus the simplest definition of grace is what is clearly beyond the power of a human being to accomplish; and, given that our salvation is, uniquely, a change which transforms our

---

[1] *The Catechism of the Catholic Church*, paragraph number 2005; hence, CCC, 2005.

life – What is it? What is the change which brings about our salvation? Is it just a change in us? When St. Paul fell off his horse in the presence of God – in the presence of whom he discovered to be Jesus Christ – he went on to announce salvation in His name from then on. So "grace", this action of God, is orientated to who Christ is and to what His mission is; and, as with St. Paul, there is both what needs healing in each of us "to see" and what each of us, being given sight, needs to do.

In the following poems there are different accounts of what God has made possible by His action; and, indeed, it may be that we may never become completely conscious of how He has helped us. Nevertheless it may be possible to recognize that a change had a different cause: that it was impossible to marry and that, because of a particular change that was clearly not a result of either self-help or psychiatric counseling, a new beginning began to exist and unfold. In other words, there is a particular recognition of sin as a cause of our actions and that sin is not just wrongdoing but has a power to entrap us; and, therefore, salvation is not just about being able to do the good that we could not do – it is also about being freed from a trap we fell into and could not get out of.

DENATURED

As we grow up we may not understand that an action changes a person; indeed, it may not be very clear to us for a long time that this is so: that just as the man who digs the ground changes it, so he grows tired in the course of his work, so what we do generally has an effect on the world as well as changing us. Similarly, we may not have been very conscious of our ideas about love, being formed as we grew up by experiences that we may not have thought through; and, in a way, we may be passing through life as if we are on a bus or a tube: not really aware of the reality of our relationships with people. We might have tried psychological help, books and indeed conversations – but there was a deeper truth to discover, namely, that of being a sinner in need of a Saviour.

Thus "Denatured" looks at the many changes that we may go through, many of which are unfitting us for life and marriage; and, therefore, that there comes a point when God meets us where we are, loves us as we are and takes us where we cannot go without Him.

DENATURED
proteins and enzymes
are temperature-changed
to the point of damaging
what was given into a dis-ordering
disruption of
shaping, fitting functions
that belong in a soupy
process producing
healthy changes.

Deep within the heart bursts the hope
of a brilliantly beautiful,
sparklingly fresh,
undying love.

But

dazzling

look-a-like-loves,

play like mirages upon the pained senses,

as a turn through the streets raises the question:

to go in or to walk away?

A clear "no" in the conscience

is scrambled in going through the door-of-no-return,

unraveling a hitherto still struggling growing

against secret,

shameful pleasures,

dashing a youthful enthusiasm for romantic love,

as the promise of beauty

suffers a withering,

shriveling recoil,

and petals drop

to pits that would be plunged

if they were waste.

Freedom's failure is finalized in a fettered future

slowly slipping out of the delightful disguises

in which hopes of love dressed-up incomplete giving

until it is clear that what was incompletely given

has shackled the giver to a compulsively

incomplete living.

The Wisdom of the Church
communicating the wholesome nature of love
as-a-gift-to-be-given in a moment's promise
unfolding a life-time's loving is like

thumping on the chest
of a man suffering a heart attack;
who, if he survives, knows that the cause is untreated
and the complaint will recur and return.

Neither is it enough
to go in and out of the Church through the confession of sins,
turning the whole thing into a turnstile or a revolving door as,
one day in and another day out.

Failure forms a future
of being unable to pass through the matrimonial gate –
as if the fear of suffering was like
facing into the bared teeth of a beast
through which it was impossible to pass.

On the edge of falling,
I fell where only God
meets the person going down
with the grace
that bear us up –
because believing in His help
turned falling into rising.

Christ opened the hope of His help,
where only fearing the future was left,
unfastening fear's trap
that trapped me in the trappings of love
but denied me entrance to the
cross and resurrection
that awaits the matrimonial
martyrdom.

And just as the river-waters run dirty in-flood,
when the rain drenched hills wash down
so selfishness streams into the light
and bleeds the blindness
from living alone

opening the possibility of love
between us: as if the very deformity
of what was changed in the losing
has become a kind of blooming
gift of grace shining through
the wreckage of relation-less
loving.

BOILING

There are times in a marriage when we may have thought that we made a mistake in marrying the person we did; indeed, it may be that because of our history we almost think, all the time, that another wife or husband would have been better. The problem, however, is not that we suffer these thoughts and temptations; rather, the problem is that we do not humble ourselves and ask for forgiveness and help. There is a reality to the gift of marriage that is designed to show us the limit of our love; and, indeed, it may do so early on, even on the first night.

This is because marriage needs the help it is given in being a sacrament of Christ's love for His Church; and, in being a sacrament, marriage is an outward sign of a love which goes on loving through the death of marriage: through the death of discovering that my wife does not talk as much as I would like or that my husband's working life is a failure. In other words there is a patient grace, or gift of God, in making possible that persevering love which discovers, not just that there is a problem in the roots of the marriage – but that the problem is not whether or not there is enough communication in the marriage but whether or not we understand the reason for it. Thus, after many years of marriage, it began to grow on me that conversation needs the complementary help of praying together; and, therefore, the reason for there being times between us when talking was either slow or difficult was that it gave a "space" between us for the help of God to show itself.

Whether it is my own marriage or the marriage of others, difficulties are there to develop us – not because we are weak and need to be strong but because our weakness is the opportunity God needs to make His strength's home in us.

BOILING

begins

in the kitchen

where sitting in the sunshine shows

the dirty marks on the windows

contrasting the light and dark

of the declining cold-yolk-sun and the wintry,

losing-leaf-tree-bareness,

blackening,

whilst the sky colors into water-washed mauves

deepening as it darkens out of reach of the setting sun.

Sun shining through changing leaves,

running through greens to yellowing browns and reds,

steppingstones to marrying one beautiful morning,

are suddenly bare,

baring the plain branches of everyday living,

becoming like signposts

signaling what is struggling to survive:

Talking is a type of touching and

touching a type of talking;

but when both are silent

there wanes the wooing song

as it crackles like failing signals

turning communication into

interacting irritations

on the domestic radio.

And spiked talking
and pointedly touching
interfere with keeping
in contact.

When all speech
is like needless needling
and no comment can pass between
husband and wife
but that it brings closer,
the widening, wintry,
spacious leaflessness
blown through with chilling criticism,
it looks as if the marriage tree
is dying –

but prayer is a silent way of speaking,
starting afresh the simplicity of loving
"you as you are"
while walking without talking
opens the possibility
of bringing together
what being together sprung apart:
as if repulsion
is the "polar" opposite of attraction –
"the-force-of-us-driving-apart"

the gift that unites.

But down the years of marriage and family life,
beneath the busyness of too much to do in too little time,
tormented through tiredness,
an isolation grows between husband and wife,
like erosion under the road,
like love boiling dry in the daily grip
of a weeping kind of weariness,
wherein illness and an inability to communicate,
like an outer-space-inhabited inaccessibility
breaks upon the heart
a loneliness in the heart of the marriage:
an experience incommunicable:
a place unintelligible to the other.

What whirling temptations
arise in the smile of others,
their conversational cleverness
and obvious attractiveness!

But within the mystery
of Christian marriage
there is a healing place
in Mary's experience
of suffering a share in the
suffering of her Son;

and, being understood,

in the "aloneness"[2] of love,

love is nurtured to new beginnings

beyond the disappointments of

being understood:

being enveloped in the Love

that begets love.

When talking is listening

and touchingly tender

then closeness is closer

than contact and called

fruitful-union.

Love

loves begetting

new beginnings

or it is not love;

and love would not be love

if we did not need

Love to love;

and Love would not

Love in us

if Love did not first

---

[2] "Sola a sola" is a song written and sung by Kiko Arguello, a founding catechist of the *Neocatechumenal Way*, about the experience of Mary, the Mother of the Lord.

love us[3].

CHANGING

Change may be something that we thought we could go through, taking one decision or another to bring about what we thought we needed; but, as time and history showed, all I changed was what I did, where I went and who I was with. In other words there is an externality to what I changed, and changed many times. But there were changes which, thinking I could reform my own behavior, were in fact a deterioration owing to a kind of law of what becomes of seeking to save myself. So the changes I made went on destroying the life I lived, the relationships went on breaking down and courses and plans continued to be incomplete and unraveling.

But the change Christ brought about was a change which changed everything. While living in a basement flat, in front of yet another failed relationship and wondering about whether it was possible to go on or not, to go on living or not, to go on hoping when hope seemed like the faint smoke of an extinguished candle, God visited me with faith: with the belief that He existed and comes to help. This change was utterly beyond me and yet drew upon my very existence and made possible a new beginning that was like a spring bubbling up out of the ground and watering what was hidden so that it began to develop.

Thus the change Christ founded went on to be the foundation of other changes which, together with the *word of God*, continued to be incremental in a way that really brought a difference to how I am able to live marriage and family life.

---

[3] Cf. 1 John 4: 19: 'We love, because he first loved us.'

CHANGING

Coming out of living alone
into marriage is like
materializing out of space
and discovering that walls are solid
and that a particle passing through the world
is very different from being
a husband and a father.

Like an invisible force-field
around the space reserved
for himself is the man who,
marrying later in life,
finds that his children
keep quashing his domain,
bashing into the force-field,
and stepping on his plans
for that perfect peace
in which he will finish his work
and refresh himself
before pressing on.

But they
keep taking his time
and filling the house with
noise and activity when,
unable to hide,

he is plagued by
button-pressing gadgets
being pressed into service
relentlessly.

A turning point in the tide of
time-ceasing-to-be-my-own
was the onslaught of homecoming; and,
instead of demanding back
the quiet after their return,
I started to stop dreading their return
and to help them relax
after school!

Instead of the ever hoped for
escape of driving the spaceship into
an extra-terrestrial orbit,
taxi-dad became a
positive boarding experience
between father and child
as they navigated their way
through communication instead
of complaintification: a kind of diseased
undoing of the father-child relationship
by which he objected to whatever they did.
whether before, on or after
returning home.

Wherein lay the secret change
that changes still if not in the
changing prayer for all
their constant
needs?

Losing
time was found
to be finding time to help;
giving lifts was being given
opportunities to hear news and to talk;
and picking up what was dropped
was dropping one more cause
for criticism.

Change
involved a change
in who had to change;
and, indeed, while I hoped
that the other will change,
the first to be changed
is to be me.

YOU AND I

The *Neocatechumenal Way*, which is a formation in adult
Christian Faith, which I had once left and to which I returned, has
given us many opportunities to go away with the Lord to a quiet place;

and, over the years, there have been very many different times when we went to listen, to pray and to be with others who are also on this walk.

It has been, and still is, one of the wonders that the Lord has worked in our lives as, with a growing family, we always managed to find babysitters or, taking the children with us, we were helped with babysitters "*in situ*". There were certainly occasions when the organization entailed in getting away was intensely difficult; however, prayer and perseverance were called forth from us and were rewarded by the help we needed. What makes this clearer is that when my parents wanted to go on "retreat" as a young married couple with small children my mother stayed behind; but then, when the playpen broke, she got on the bus and went too: it being easier to go than to stay behind with a broken playpen! This was almost the only time they got away for a retreat when we were growing up. In other words, there is no doubt that the Lord has transformed the situation for us through the characteristics of this way.

Now that many years have passed, we are still called to go away to a quiet place with the Lord and, whether it is to receive a word to help us in our marriage, with our children or to know what our "mission" is, these times with the Lord are irreplaceable.

YOU AND I
walked awhile around the path
without the children with us,
the two of us,
in-between listening,
touched, as it were, by a spoken word

as much human as divine,
enriched with an insight
sensing out the significance of events
given,
like moisture
materializing out of the air

praying as we walked the morning path
around the glittering grass

when suddenly I saw the dew drops,
tipping the top of
each
singular stalk of grass,
neither bending the blade under it,
nor appearing at any other point
than that of its very peak

on which balances the lightly lit droplet of water,
implacably placed atop the very pointed end of the tip,
more precise than human hands could place it
and more numerous across the countless greens
than can be counted –
all a-glistening in the morning light.

How many times we have walked
this path of prayer and never seen this sight
in the same way as we did that day.

What lit the outside
if not the grace-giving materializing out of the
retreat-to-advance withdrawal from family life to receive
a word which framed the moment's need to see
how many times the Lord has visited me
and how many times His visit came to nothing

\-   but then He came again and
passed through the previous visits which came to nothing
and remained:

He came persistently to me
making it possible to be prayerfully
persistent in going to others!

AFTERMATH

The very word evokes a "battle" but not, in this case, the battle of weapons but, rather, the battle of words and emotions and challenges of communication.

Christmas was coming and I began looking forward to it with an expectation of God coming to act, as with the Incarnation, as with my life; however, as Christmas approached and began so did illness, both that of my children and my own. I had been looking forward to everyone being home, especially our daughter who is away at the moment; but, also, I was not looking forward to all the clearing up and helping and motivating that entails. An operation of three years ago has left me with a weakness and, occasionally, there is bleeding in the bladder; but, while it generally stops after a while, this time it went on for a week. In between all this there were also upsets and the holiday challenges of being constructively occupied.

Owing to my own weakness, I was not able to help as much as I had expected. On the other hand, I enjoyed some of the table games; and, as well, some of the unexpected helpfulness that made clearing our unused toys and books from the playroom a reality. The pre-Christmas vegetable chopping had gone very well. On Christmas Eve we went to Church, walking, cycling and by car, even with the one who had been working; and, therefore, Christmas morning was more relaxed than expected and it began, as usual, with a short gathering in front of the crib, with a reading, hymns and prayers and ending with a present under the chair!

What gave it a sense of "battle", then, was all the in between times when we hoped to keep everyone together without, at the same time, stifling or burdening anyone; and, therefore, it was hard at times to see how to keep the peace and address what was going on without becoming acrimonious and grumpy.

"Aftermath" sums up the sense that although Christmas often seems to be for the children, the reality of life frequently helps me to see that I need a savior.

AFTERMATH

is a time

of grey-limb bareness:

of cold taking down the leaves

and leaving the branches to begin again

in the spring;

and, at the same time, a transparency
comes to land as
trees await the foliage which fills out
the spaces and transforms
the distances between
here and the space beyond.

Suffering
bites a-purpling asphyxiation,
downing meanness and,
in the hiding heart,
homes in on being a victim

or

in some secret, graced and subtle way,
almost like an interior drip that hooks
us up to the "Life" we need

it sows
a simplicity like winter landscapes,
a startling nakedness,
even to our own eyes:

of simply being irritated by everyone in a different way,
unable to accept an aspect of each person around,
almost suffocating in the presence of an antagonism
which is simply present in the presence of others.

But there is no antidote in the spiky interactions,
as if blistering in the sun is sunbathing,
and so, seeking the cooler, softer emollient of a breeze
to turn contact from that frictionizing over-sensitivity
to sympathy:

to being-with
my-brothers-and-sisters-in-life
there is the graced begetting gentleness
going beyond and above
and beside and around
and through the

wrenching, raw and wretched heart
which, souring, stinks and shrinks without it.

Wintry landscapes show,
through their cold glow,
a transparent neediness
for growth!

The
boxing of the decorations,
eating leftover sweets and puddings,

taking down the tree, cut by cut and bagging up
branch by dried branch of loosened, still green needles,
sharp and insensitive to my touch,

unable to take water although watered,
constantly conscious of the growing possibility
of a blazing fire of dried resin branches
dripping with the immenseness of a moment
when a fire might leap and consume
all too rapidly what is a room

and turning towards work and school,
is about answering the question:

What was that about?

Bungling relationships,
illness, the weariness of life,
fears and failures, poverty and debts,
admitting a kind of appalling
pain of a life-decaying
neediness, almost
needling, stabs of regret
pointing
if I will only see

to the need for a savior.

The
aftermath
of Christmas is discovering
that Christ comes to help me in the searching

out of the wisdom of love

in the everyday life

of a husband, dad

and writer.

GUEST POET AND POEM: ANNABELLE MOSELEY

Annabelle Moseley is an American poet and author of ten books, including *Sacred Braille: The Rosary as Masterpiece.* She is host of the podcasts on Sacramental Living: "Then Sings My Soul," and "Destination: Sainthood," on WCAT Radio. Moseley is one of five Catholic artists profiled in the 2019 Documentary Film, *Masterpieces*, about the vocational call of the arts.

Moseley has won the titles of Walt Whitman Birthplace Writer in-Residence (2009-2010) and 2014 Long Island Poet of the Year. She is a Professor of Theology, teaching at St. Joseph's Seminary and St. Joseph's College in Long Island, where she lives with her husband and children. She writes, "The vocation of writing in the Catholic tradition, as I see it, *transcends* the act of writing and becomes a way of seeing the world: a life's work of transforming pain into purpose. It is having a sacramental eye in both the way one writes and the way one lives, and being attuned to the beauty and sorrow therein not for its own sake, but as a summons to God."

"A PRAYER FOR SETTING THE TABLE":
An introduction by the author Annabelle Moseley

The House of the Sacred Heart

"The task the Lord Jesus has given me is – the task of testifying to the good news of God's grace" (Acts 20:24)

When I was a child, you could say I became a student of grace. Beginning at ten years old, and for several years, during our family's most sorrowful mysteries, I found myself in my grandmother's home even more than my own, eating there multiple times a week, even living there for a time. It was a sanctuary, that epic house. How may I begin to describe it— outside, it was painted a deep red, like the color of the Sacred Heart, and it was a pulsing thrum of life to the many who entered, with a white picket fence out front; and cowbells clattering with rollicking joy when you opened the door. The rooms were filled with whimsical antiques and classic religious art; and the kitchen was always ready to welcome whomever dropped by. I used to watch the care with which my grandmother prepared a meal; the way she always made more than she needed in case someone in the family stopped by unexpectedly (and someone often did); the way she always set a table with great attention to detail even for a humble meal. She consistently brought dignity and love to the act of eating, wise and warm conversation, and wholesome food served on blue willow plates.

The Catechism of the Catholic Church defines grace as, "favour, the free and undeserved help that God gives us to respond to his call to become children of God, adoptive children, partakers of the divine nature and of eternal life." And so grace is free, undeserved help that enables us to respond to our calling to help build and dwell forever in God's Kingdom. The red house made me want to become a builder of what I was a witness to there, and dwell forever in the place its strong foundation and humble walls anticipated.

Grace is granted when we witness its most resplendent power on our life's transfiguring mountains. But it's also there, even in the storm before the fourth watch of the night, the kind of storm I lived through while taking refuge in the red house. It was there I learned that when things are at their darkest, when we can't hear God's voice over the wind, we can train our ear to listen for the sound of the sacred whisper. For whether we walk across angry waves all the way to Christ's arms or grab for his hand just before we sink under the sea, the gift of grace is equally lavish. My grandmother's house was the beating heart of the family even during the storm: her children visiting from their varied paths. My grandmother would lead us all in discussions of faith, literature, theology, and frequent family stories of the brave generations before. I learned my family's history and saw the recurring pattern, as in scripture: triumph came through faith, every time.

One of the greatest epic poems is *The Odyssey*. Our hero, Odysseus, learns after his journeys to both harrowing and enticing locales, that the most important journey is the one home. It's one of the richest discoveries we can make: our eternal home in heaven is the end-goal. To quote St. Therese of Lisieux, "The world's thy ship and not thy home." But a noble quest in this life is to make a place to live that reminds one of heaven; neither a house impressive for the sake of impressing, nor a convenient place to hang your hat, but a dwelling place so filled with goodness and deeper meaning that anyone who enters can feel something special there, perceive the poetry of daily life, and long to return. It is a worthy ambition to pray for the grace to make a home that on its humble scale — anticipates heaven.

Because of the love and the lessons learned within it, my grandmother's red house became a legend to which I always wanted to find my way back. When my grandmother moved out of her house to move in with my aunt, I began to have a recurring dream about returning to the red house. I would dream of breaking in through a window and finding it just as it had been when she'd lived there. I'd be back at that kitchen table again, while she poured the tea. Other times, I'd dream the house was empty and I was filling it once more with the furniture she had given away.

Over fifteen years after my grandmother moved out of the red house, and just one year after her death, my uncle purchased and moved into it, and set about restoring the charm and beauty of the family's heart. After much mourning of her death, I was given the grace of returning, of entering under that roof again, this time with my husband and our children. I brought my family to visit the sacred place that had for so long been just a memory. I leaned against its walls, and recalled the words of St. Therese: "If I cannot see the brilliance of your Face or hear your sweet voice, O my God, I can live by your grace, I can rest in your Sacred Heart!"

A PRAYER FOR SETTING THE TABLE
for Annabelle Black, in honor of her 100th Birthday

As the tablecloth unfurls like an altar linen,
as napkins are folded and cups are placed

with the dishes of ordinary time—
I pray for you, to be like you.
It isn't always in words.
Sometimes, the motion of my fingers is the prayer
over the Rosary of daily tasks—
smoothing folds of fabric, scraping pots,
polishing kitchen sacramentals.

You know the way the room breathes—
as bowls are taken out and put away?
Of course you know it well—
The thrum of daily devotions.
You've always been one for doing, pursuing—
moving forward.

Yet you are our table and we sit around you.
We pray to nourish others the way you nourish us.
For our tables to welcome, food sustain,
to have enough left for the guests we do not expect—
for our words to anoint like oil.

Here is something I have never told you:
Those many childhood nights I ate at your table,
where life's mysteries were broken and shared—
I studied the blue willow plates
you set each night.
Even during the worst winter,
my fork swept potatoes, gravy, bits of savory meat
and uncovered a story.

Cast in the familiar pattern,
there were pagodas, fences, shining waterways
and a boat with a figure searching the horizon.
But what kind of wind made the willow fronds splay so far apart?
Who were the three figures holding lanterns on a bridge?
Each night I told myself a different tale
found hope in the pair of birds, above it all—
larger than the strife below.

You fed me from willow-patterned dishes
when I didn't think I could eat,
when my father was dying
and daffodils were frozen under snow.
But always on your plates
flying above this relentless searching—
two birds, facing each other, wings arched in triumph.
That winter, in blue and white patterns,
the Holy Spirit, in its many-feathered glory
descended
on each dish
you placed before me.

This is how you've always fed your family.
Even now, as our tablecloth unfurls like an altar linen,
as napkins are folded and cups are placed
with the dishes of ordinary time—
We pray for you, to be like you.
It isn't always in words.

Part V: The Sacraments

Why do sacraments even exist? This is why the sacraments exist: they are integral to creation's return to the Creator. The loss of the originally splendid gift of creation being in harmony with creatures is evidenced all around us in the multiple, multiplying tragedies of disruption, disorder and sin; indeed, this is expressed in a searing and wounded relationship between each and all of us and God which, if it remains untreated, severs life from Life and opens an appalling, uncrossable chasm, between eternal life and the undyingness of an everlasting death.

So what is a sacrament and how is it possible to write about it? In one sense, it could be argued, that to write about the sacraments of the Catholic, Christian Church, is to write about the intangible: "grace *escapes our experience* and cannot be known except by faith" (CCC, 2005[1]); however, it is in the very nature of the sacraments to be so ordered as for there to be "an outward sign of an inward grace". Thus, while not proposing to write about all the sacraments, it is sufficient to say that there is a living imagery in the very fact that what is involved in a particular sacrament, whether it be ritual, matter, words or whatever is characteristic of human love, healing or service, is taken

---

[1] *The Catechism of the Catholic Church*, paragraph number 2005; hence, CCC, 2005.

up into the sacrament itself. Specifically, as with the sacrament of baptism water, the pouring of it and the words used to confer it, are taken up into the original work of the Creator, Redeemer and Sanctifier. God, in the mystery of divine creativity, takes up again the very nature of His creation and recreates us through incorporation, as it were, in the very mystery of the *Incarnation of the word of God from the very beginning* fulfilled fully in *the Word made flesh* (Jn. 1: 14). In the providential moment in which God acts He turns time through the timelessness of the Son of God towards everlasting life.

What, then, can we say of the turning through time of the recovery of creation's participation in the gift of creation?

BREAD OF LOVE, WINE OF GLORY

"Bread of Love, Wine of Glory"[2] is about an inexplicable love; indeed, love is perhaps only explicable as love: a kind of intelligibility which is only intelligible to a lover.

Of all the mysteries of life, the mystery of Love made flesh in Jesus Christ takes us beyond our own definition of love; indeed, who would have thought that it is possible that God would make of Himself a gift, literally, for us to consume in communion?

What measurement of love is possible if we begin to see that God is not remote, on high, unreachable – but is so close as to take into Himself all our pain? That the nails in the hands and feet, the pierced side, the scourging and the crown of thorns are, literally, how Jesus

---

[2] Published in *Second Spring*, Issue One, 2001, p. 20: secondspring.co.uk; and, also, in the book, The Family on Pilgrimage: God Leads Through Dead Ends (https://enroutebooksandmedia.com/familyonpilgrimage/).

Christ has taken the pain and suffering of our lives into His very flesh; and, in so doing, shows us that His love is an embrace beyond our understanding: that His love takes us into Himself in a way that we cannot adequately image. In coming to communion, however, we livingly enter into the salvation He gives us as we, simultaneously, give Him who we are in the very imperfection of our vesseled being. In the dialogue of this reciprocal exchange of gifts we can beg His help as He gives Himself to us: in a giving of Himself as humble as it is unreserved; for, if He has not refused the gift of Himself, why would He not listen to us to whom He comes so humblingly close?

BREAD OF LOVE, WINE OF GLORY

The Firebird
consumes to God
Christ's asphyxiation.

The Son's
threshed-pressed
separating soul
arose like incense
off His Body's cracked
Blood and Water.

Christ-risen
for our forgiveness,
carries back to man
the Dovetailed sign

of the cross
on dry land.
In the marriage
of that fledgling monument
God-made-man made of Himself a meal:

Bride and Groom
open Their lips
in fertile prayer;

and the Father's Breath
settles like a kiss
on our gifts.

The Mother in God
broods over the
fruits of His earth

and their being is born into the
Body and Blood of our Lord Jesus Christ:
Bread of Love, Wine of Glory,

Food for Their open-mouthed children
Drink for our thirsting through the desert
sign in our sudden flocking

and feathers to the heart

of man in flight

to the Most High.

IMMERSION

Baptism, almost the very "opening" gift of the indwelling of God and His gifts; and, I say "almost the very "opening" gift" because we cannot discount the history which goes before, either in our own lives or those who have influenced us. Baptism, then, entails the outward sign of the pouring of water three times over a person's head or his or her immersion, three times, in the river Jordan[3]; indeed, baptism "means to "plunge" or "immerse" into … water" (CCC, 1214). And the words, which accompany this action of pouring or immersing in water, are that it is done "in the name of the Father, and of the Son, and of the Holy Spirit" (CCC, 1240).

But, as with our whole lives, there is always the question: In what are we immersed? Our sufferings, disappointments, failures, griefs and the everyday pressures of living to work and working to live or not even being able to work and barely living? Are we immersed in the possibility of living life to the full and dying wholeheartedly having given everything we have got to give? Are we immersed in the mystery of the mercy of God who looks at what we have done with our lives and makes a work of art from it; indeed, are we able or not to glorify

---

[3] I say this somewhat provocatively as Christ was baptized in the Jordan and, because of this, the waters of the Jordan are forever blessed; but, in the case of any other baptism, the water needs to be blessed.

God as the Great Recycler – Who takes the rubbish of sin and transforms our life into a blessing greater than the regret of rubbishing it?

IMMERSION
is standing in the head-high shadow
of blasting speakers in a semi-lit hall
of almost inaudibly speaking people,
moving between "place" and "place"
and the activities of the day:
an almost horizontal burial
in upstanding positions.

Being baptized is being
immersed in sacred waters and words,
descending into the mysteriously living
liturgical depths of the life and death,
dying and rising of Jesus Christ:
a bath in which bathing
is a descent into the cross'
crucifixion of sin.

"What has been driven into my hands
are not the nails but the pains of the world poised
between powerlessness and the impossibility
of climbing out of the trapped, crushed places
when we fall and fail."

"What has been driven into my side
is not the lancing, slicing, slitting cut of the spear
but the broken bonds of marriage and family life."

"What has been driven into my feet is not the nails
but the sin that stops us walking".

The baptismal walk started
in the immersive setting
in which the impulse of grace
started a listening to the calling Lord

who calls throughout the falling times,
the wounded and discouraging years,
across the hopeless wastes,

to strive for the star-bright wisdom of ages,
in the company of a pilgrim people,

having begun a sonship,
started a relationship,
to which God is unfathomably
faithful.

REGENERATIVE

The theme of this poem was suggested by a catechesis, that is a
formative account of an aspect of our faith, on what the *Sacrament of*

Reconciliation is; it was written by the late Carmen Hernandez, one of the founders of the *Neocatechumenal Way*: a process of post-or-pre-baptismal formation in an adult Christian Faith. The essential point of this catechesis was that for the Jewish people the forgiveness of God was like being regenerated in the depths of God. Thus God, from the very generative dynamism of His inner life – regenerates the people that He forgives. Perhaps it is even possible to speak of the human heart being regenerated in the depths of the Church's rejuvenating merciful embrace: as if forgiveness is a kind of dynamiting the old nature and bringing in the new – all of which lies latent-to-be-drawn upon in the baptismal gift of being called to be formed in the likeness of Christ.

Nevertheless, it is still possible to receive this sacrament as if it is like scrubbing off a bit of discoloration: as if the death and resurrection of Christ is not the preeminent "form" through which we will be transfigured, little by little, until the unbelievable event of the *Second Coming* of Jesus Christ. At the same time there have been moments when, almost insistently, we have been driven to find a confessor: a priest who will hear and help us with discerning advice. However, in another sense, confession is not a singular act but a process of letting God enlighten us about the help we need; and, therefore, listening to the word of God unseals the voice of conscience: opening a dialogue between the word of God and our everyday inter-reactive reality.

In general, then, confession can both take us through our own history and the uncovering of resentments and blindnesses of the past but it can also help us to recognize the ongoing rivalries and tendencies which flare up, in the present, obstructing the good we would do to another as if, suddenly, a fire has broken out between us. More importantly, however, confession is like the excavation of a well: the more we recognize and confess our sins the more the love of God wells up in us: "I tell you that her sins, her many sins, must have been forgiven her, or she would not have shown such great love" (Lk. 7: 47)

REGENERATIVE
medicine is when the inward parts,
having degenerated or, in some way, shriveled,
are in the very process of being regrown.

As if the very immersion of baptism
percolates through the hardened arteries,

of a prayer-slack dearth of good deeds,

bursting upon the almost insensible conscience
sensing something in the crises of life.

Confession can be like a car-clean:
efficient for what is obvious,
almost slotting it in in-between
shopping and the busyness of the day.

Or confession is like plunging,
falling fully conscious,
or diving deeply

into the digestive juices of the *word,*

uncovering more fully the fullness of being loved
enough to be opened to receive the salt-gritting

of a welcoming new nature

that dissolves edifying gifts
in the inedible, rejectable and indigestible
waste:
opening the closed hand
in acts of generosity and forming
an inwardly pearly brightness.

And then the outward sign of falling to the knees
expresses the pattern of forgiveness
rising, like a thermal, from the
uplifting waves of the risen,
crucified Christ

breaking out a newness,
from the old-new man
freshly found in the hands of Christ:

the transient beauty of a graced love
bearing an eternally resplendent
change of what is feebly porous
into what is magnificently permeated by a
lasting happiness.

Walking with others
helps us to walk in remembrance
of all who have gone before us,
helping us to remember all who
are around us and who will
see our trail and, possibly, tread after us,
perhaps running up and wondering
if they can come too.

Confession turns our inwardness outward
in the hope that God's blessings will befall others
because of witnessing to the renewing
He is doing with us.

PART I: A RINGED PAIR

Marriage, like the nature of life itself, both repeats and repeats unrepeatably the mystery of individually replicating a universally common pattern of reciprocal self-giving. There is no doubt that, from the beginning, marriage heralds one of the greatest mysteries of human being: that man, male and female, and perhaps particularly in the mystery of marriage mirroring an eternal mystery, makes present in an unmistakable way the simplicity of a visible expression of the Blessed Trinity: the eternal communion from all eternity of the unoriginated God the Father, the ever-only begotten Son of God and the proceeding of the Holy Spirit from and through the Father and the Son. Indeed, it may well be one of the greatest reasons for rejoicing that, on entering eternal bliss, each man and woman discovers the particular way that they are made in the image and likeness of God.

As regards my own vocation to marriage, suffice it to say here that it is a time-delayed present of grace: that, in the gifting of God, there is a slow discovery of the greatness of this gift – going, as it does, to the depths of undoing the harm of habitual loneliness and hidden selfishness; and, therefore, it is one of the greatest tragedies of life that people do not cling to Christ in clinging to each other to the point of living beyond the poverty, the problems, the illness, the crises and the coming of children so fully that they smash into the secret selfishness – such that we come to an almost serene thanksgiving for what we have received and go on receiving in the unfolding of family life[4].

A RINGED PAIR,
bride and groom take flight together:

flying in the formation
of Christ and His Church,

great winged,
intertwining, twirling, twisting flight paths,

---

[4] I have written elsewhere, in *Scripture: A Unique Word,* the trilogy on *Truth from truth* (all published by Cambridge Scholars Publishing) in *The Human Person: A Bioethical Word, The Family on Pilgrimage: God Leads Through Dead Ends,* in *The Prayerful Kiss* (all published by En Route Books and Media) of the concrete experiences that are also touched upon in Part II of this book. This particular introduction is also indebted to the thoughts that arose in an interview with Annabelle Moseley on the first volume of this collection: *The Prayerful Kiss,* located on WCAT Radio in two parts at https://www.spreaker.com/user/wcatradio/destination-sainthood-ep08 and https://www.spreaker.com/user/wcatradio/destination-sainthood-ep09.

turning through time and spreading outwards
just as they draw on ever widening roots in the course
of remembering their histories

rippling out in a multitude of directions,
flitting in and out of various flocks.

"Watch out for the shadowing birds of prey":

Desert! Be unfaithful! Abandon all hope!

Abounding in the deserted places of
illnesses, hardships, silences,
poverty and problems
with the children!

Following,
in the very vicissitudes of flight,
the shaping influence of the Bride and Groom,

soaking in the sun that lights their way through space,
drawing them on

to turn around and through
the arc of transformation,
trailing others they have influenced,
following the sky-trail left by those

already passing into eternity.
The quantum leap began even before
each received a triple pouring of water across the forehead
in obedience to Christ and in the company of His Church,

a triple immersion in the passion and rising of Christ,
and then, at a favorable time, discovering
through discernment and the evidence of events
how unfit for each other is each for the other
that God, the Creator of all,

recreates them both as Adam is to Eve
and the Church is to Christ.

Traveling slowly, day by day,
through the chores that rub into sores
as working at work is multiplied by work in the home,
rawifying romance into service,

like cords into rope,
grate and fire into hearth
and flames and food into
heating a home
and feeding a family.

Growing grey but the grey days die
in the course of a life fully lived ending loneliness
in the gift of marriage and the company

of children and innumerable others.
Growing old amidst the growing older
is a new round of discovering
the gifts of each and the calling of all

to unfold fully the fullness of life
bursting upon others,
like the flowers of spring,
or the drops that fall from fully soaked living,
raising the hopes of all
that the word of God brings
imperceptible changes,
lightening the load,
leading back to the Son
from which we all dropped
in the moment of existing.

Approaching eternity
is like brightening to the point
that stains, discoloring in the heat, burn
until the brightness changes them.

Communion,
like atomic fuel,
propels us through
the daily cross in everyday suffering
bearing the promise from the moment of immersion
of being transfigured through

the transfiguring glory of God:
The pattern of falling and rising
repeated *en route*
renewing the first immersive
forgiveness in us

flinging the witnesses
we were called to be
of the ringed,
redeeming love,
into an unfathomably
unimaginably rippling eternity

resounding with man,
male and female,
echoing the mystery
of the Blessed Trinity.

PART II: WHIRLPOOLS

Using a touched cup, a used plate, food another has left, putting the knife in the butter and then in the jam are a number of the ways in which our sensitivity shows itself; either we risk being too careless and being unhygienic or we are too careful and risk being obsessively clean. Underlying these different possibilities are all the characteristics of everyday ways of doing things and whether or not we verge on the obsessive or careless; but then, in the intense moments of life, when we are overrun with the needs of others or the tasks of the day, there is a tendency for the currents that run within our everyday behavior to become supercharged. Thus, when it comes to a viral epidemic it may be that our spouse, or one of our children, will be overcome with one of the many possible fears that lie, as it were, fitfully sleeping – but then awakes like an echo of a natural disaster, disturbing everyday life and challenging the possibility of retaining its routines.

WHIRLPOOLS
turn us to the tipping edge
screwing down like the water
twisting through the plug hole.

Currents come together,
turning, opening, pouring down
and around without abating.

Tendencies to depression,
fear of wide-spreading illnesses,
vulnerable people,

isolation,

conflate in the imagination
and threaten reason.

On the tipping edge
of the whirling
is the temptation to go:

to abandon the place
from which pulling exerts
its awful influence
as a lightless hopelessness
has the hapless fruit

of hoping for the help
of death.

Distress
makes my wife
unreachable:

her unreachability
opens my limited
reach upon the
limitless
One.

Darkness breaks
in front of the matchless
help of prayer

and sitting
in the garden sunlight
begets a priceless
recognition of facts

which,
like a bridge,
lead to stepping
beyond the scope
of fear's dwelling
gloom.

But the pre-dinner slump
and the indoor pottering
revives the clamor
of imagination's
pointed claim of the
possibility of being
spreading disease,

suffocating reason's
grasp of health
and happiness

in a recurring grip
of relentless
decline.

The cycle
returns

but
I need

help to rebuff
fear's binding
blindness

and so I
pray again,
and again remind her
again of the times
and places of other
fearful fears and
beg hope's help
again.

As she descends again,
I pray again,
naming another
to reach like a shore
upon which to beach.

Grace
opens the
inside door
and my wife
steps outside
again.

Part I: The Priest-Shepherd

It is a hard time to be a priest because the public perception has been blighted by the reality of sin; and, whether it is a personal experience or not, it is a total contradiction of a priestly vocation to trap those who come for help. There is no doubt an ongoing work of addressing the various dimensions of what turns a welcoming greeting into a criminal act.

In these times the work of renewal is as urgent as ever and, in the light of these events, ever more urgent. Thus the Good Shepherd's work is not only bringing into the open what is hidden, healing the hurt and offence of what has been done – but of undermining the very origin of the vice that has grown instead of the virtue: of supplanting the ugliness of a disfigured humanity with the beauty of beholding through grace the transformation of it.

Each one of us knows the many, innumerable times that we have benefited from the ministry of a priest; and, indeed, more than benefited but actually been helped to renounce the louse infested habits that infected us and, inseparably, our relationships. There are many times that maybe even a superficial help helped to prevent a more serious sin; and, in so far as it was possible, the minister contributed to undoing the hold of the slavemaster's grip and gave us, yet again, another opportunity to get beyond his wrenching, ripping and gnawing reach.

In the end, without being blinded by indifference, bigotry or the blight of offense, we need to see afresh the human face that Christ Himself gave to His ministry among us.

THE SHEPHERD

comes to a wandering,
travel weary sheep,
pausing, unexpectedly, lamp raised,
beside an almost sleeping traveler,
resting on the floor of a cottage in the mountains,
water running from a stream above
and no electric lighting to hide the dark,
wondering about the purpose of life,
remembering a few people sat on rocks in the river
in the day before below,
exploring naturalism:

the Shepherd pauses, lamp raised,
the traveler falls in the presence
of the passing Shepherd:
still; silent; but here,
where all is still and dark in the night.

Morning broke in the valley as I sat –
expecting what? Who? Wondering what it meant
and although becoming entangled in entangling thoughts
I started searching only to find myself on a long road,
almost losing it many times, but

the Shepherd visited in various ways and always left,
leaving a restless searching and a searching restlessness.

Many shepherds, like bystanders,
offer a drink, food, a little lightening of the load,
but then, slipping into obscurity, banality,

or worse,

grasp at the pilgrim from the slimy hole
in which they have fallen fast.

A variety of shepherds
grapple with the love that wrestles with them
to make the gift of making the Shepherd's presence
more fully visible.

Timeless shepherd's shape the present from the past,
ever opening on the day's work,
whether in the home, across the city, the countryside
or by being transmitted in word and deed,
picture or preaching,
here and throughout the world.
Priceless shepherds
take us to the Shepherd:

who breaks a word on the ground,
in the mess and slimy experience of trashed lives,
baking out of it a cup and a plate for the bearing of gifts

as if the power of a proclaimed word

is followed by a cool breeze
in which the opening of our heart is almost
grazed, gently, by a change only God makes possible,
as if the word and its fruits
flow from the very source of life,

through which the
sharing of His Body and Blood builds,
because of it, a dwelling in proportion to the indwelling
Love that loves to raise the fallen

from the falling into sin,
which nails into miserableness
the dying undead

opening a beginning through a dead end.

The Shepherd who seeks His sheep
renews the shelter of the Church
in which they heal and from which they
go out in search of the last sheep,

like the last bale of the harvest,

at the end of the season, marking the end of time,
and the moment of His return:

Transfiguring liturgical Easter

into the magnificent blaze of the
Second Coming of Our Lord and Saviour
Jesus Christ.

PART II: THE DOMESTIC SHEPHERD

There are many aspects to the work of parents; but, in the end, parents give what they have received. It is essential, then, that my wife and I are formed as wholesomely as possible and that we pass on, in the family environment, a wide ranging familiarity with the many faceted nature of culture; and, at the same time, that there is a faith-enriched daily life where, in all, there is no confusion between natural and supernatural gifts: between faith and reason. What is clearly differentiated can enter into dialogue[5] and, like the oiling of a mechanism, the presence of trace elements or the touch of love, grace makes us more fruitful.

One of the characteristics of the liturgical life of marriage and family is a clear but dynamic structure to everyday life; and, therefore, while a family is not a monastery yet it needs a rhythm of both individual and common prayer. At the same time, too, the word of God comes to enlighten us about our situation and God; and, as with the word "mercy", to remind us of what St. John Paul II said: God's mercy limits evil. Whether it is the basic day, then, the distribution of chores and the discovery of both talents and cooperation, prayer is like a holy sprinkler through the day, quelling quarrels, inspiring little

---

[5] See, for example, *Scripture: A Unique Word*, Newcastle upon Tyne: Cambridge Scholars Publishing, 2014: Chapter 3; cf. *Conception: An Icon of the Beginning*, 2019.

helps or modifications of attitude or response; and, indeed, reminding us too, of Pope Francis' invitation to regularly call on the forgiveness of God.

THE DOMESTIC SHEPHERD
and his wife
are amidst their flock,
timing the day,
between sunrise and sunset,
distributing work,

gathering at mealtimes,
an empty seat needs an answer,
an unanswered phone call needs to be repeated,
a latecomer needs meeting,

looking for the missing
and helping the troubled

through the uncertain
hours.

Were we in flight we would be in formation,
were we walking we would be on pilgrimage,
were we sailing we would be a crew-in-training,
were we home we would be around the table at times,
were we away it would be time to return.

Getting up earlier and going to bed later,
the domestic shepherd takes and meets
his children in the thick of their own lives,
not losing the thread of their plans
and peopled lives.

Were we dancers we would need a choreographer,
were we footballers we would need a coach,
were we writers we would need a mentor,
were we scientists we would need experts,
were we apprentices we would need skilled workmen.

Through the many hours of life's changes,
there are many moments of listening and saying yes,
many fewer times the answer is no,
in between there are numerous conversations
about a variety of everyday activities.

Were we wounded we would need a doctor,
were we in debt we would need a benefactor,
were we without a limb we would need an aid,
were we lonely we would need companions,
were we sinners we would need a saviour.
Each day brings a task of recognizing talents
and encouraging possibilities,
disclosing vocational choices
and discernment between them,
being a multifaced member of society

and welcoming the participation
of others in the cultural wealth
of the world and the mystery
of life everlasting.

The domestic shepherd and his wife and family
are an expression of the mystery
of the Good Shepherd's fold
of domestic Churches
in the One Church of Christ.

Guest Poet and Poem: Teresa J. Herbic

Teresa Herbic is a writer, editor, and the author of six Christian books including: "Through the Fire: Healing of Cancer, Tumors, and Other Nuisances" and "Family Prayer Made Easy" in English and Spanish[6]. She is an advocate for adoption, foster and orphan care through these books by providing proceeds to children's homes, adoption, foster and orphan care causes (https://ambassador-international.com/book-author/teresa-j-herbic/).

God has blessed Teresa and her husband Galen with three precious adopted children and treasured gifts, Meyana, Braxten, and Nina, as well as a Son (Nina's husband) Stanislov and three grandchildren, Pasha, Angelina, and Milan.

---

[6] Cf. https://www.amazon.com/Teresa-J.-Herbic/e/B00IZOHX6W%3Fref=dbs_a_mng_rwt_scns_share.

"MARKS OF ETERNITY":
An Introduction by the author Teresa J. Herbic

We began growing close to the Lord and learning more of His great sacrifices around Easter. It was during a time we had chosen to adopt our first child. We had submitted all of our adoption paperwork and dossier but had not received a call about the child we would adopt.

We felt anxious and, internally, there grew an agonizing pain inside our hearts to be with our child. My husband and I pondered what to do next, and we both agreed, we will spend the entire Easter weekend worshipping and praying to God.

We thought of His sacrifice for us and how we really were not suffering at all. We were just longing for our daughter. Yet, the Lord suffered immensely and He died on the cross for our sins, leaving marks for eternity.

In God's grace, on Monday just after the Easter holiday, we received a call from our adoption agency proclaiming, we have a lovely child for you! Nine-month old Mei Yan which we soon named Meyana meaning "beautiful flower". Our whole world changed, and we were delighted at how incredibly the Lord responded.

Before we knew it, we were truly thankful to adopt a handsome son, too, named Braxten. And we were so grateful to reconnect with a third lovely child named Nina who we adopted in recent years. Our family is touched in every way by the Lord and adoption.

For His marks of eternity truly carry through to us as mercy, grace, peace, and eternal hope. Hope we now see on a regular basis as we seek the Lord more and more faithfully. Thank You Jesus for your sacrifice for us and Your precious gift of marks that last throughout eternity.

MARKS OF ETERNITY

With marks on Your Palms
Scars Deep and Wide,
Scars You Can't Hide.

For God Saw Sin,
And Sent You
As the One.

Willing to Die,
On the Rugged Cross,
In Place of our sin…

For many Lost Sheep…

Still, the World
Remains Dark, Shattered.
Hopes Die, Blood Splattered.

Temptation Stirring,
Sin from Within,
Time to Begin Again.

Jesus, We Call You,
Your Scars Deliver
Us Like a River…
Life has Purpose Now…

Serving You, God
Oh Lord, Most High
Our Hope in the Sky.

Talents, Gifts, We
Use for Your Glory,
So You Write Our Story…

Yet Marks Remain
Along with the Pain,
Still Comes the Rain.

But, Heaven Awaits…

We Reach for the Gates,
The Power of Christ Within,
Overcomes All the Sin.

Praise God for Your
Sacrifice ---For Us
to be Saved…

Thank You Jesus for
Your Marks of Eternity
That Make Us Free…

You are Our One and Only King!
Love,
Your Eternal Family

PART VI: WRITING

This book has very definitely been a writing battle; every day taking up the challenge of what to do next and, gradually, a structure emerging through the theme of nature and grace. Thus there have been very noticeable changes in the fluency, as it were, of what has been written. Indeed, it has been very evident that the prose has provided an opportunity to bring out many aspects of life, either lived personally or what people are going through in our time.

The poetry, however, although it is more like a word pattern on the page, has been much more of a struggle to write; indeed, writing the poems could almost be called "hacking them out". The whole process, from initial idea to completed piece, has been altogether very slow and often involved numerous edits and rewrites; and, while one or two of these pieces have come from what has been written before, the vast majority of the pieces have grown, one way or another, with this volume.

There is a definite contrast between writing academically, even when it involves an element or more of personal experience, and writing "The Second Collection". It is even possible to consider that, in many ways, this is an exercise in empathy, in engaging with many experiences in which there may well have been a seed of what others have suffered more severely; and, therefore, there is a kind of expansion of the imagination in which, hopefully, many people will find the starting point for their own account or, if not, will take comfort in a range of their lived experience being expressed.

WORDS TORN FROM TEARS

This began as one of those phrases that said something thought: that there are words to speak that cannot be spoken but that they are suffused with tears and soaked in sobs that make stutterers of us and give staccato pitch-spikes to our words – ranging wildly from silence to high voltage squeaks and slowly unutterable sounds. I remember, particularly, traveling to the place where Christ asked Peter "Do you love me?" and, along with many others, being asked this question; and, in the moment of answering, tears sweeping down my face and throbbing emotions stealing, unpredictably, sounds and words that were simple to say – but as if pounded by blasting, splashes of breaking waves: "Yes; I love you".

Thinking through, then, the times when it has been difficult if not impossible to speak is also a way of sharing with others that we are not plastic, *papier-mâché* or polished bronze – but blooded breathers of sufferings which should have snuffed us out.

WORDS TORN FROM TEARS

wrought and wrung from sufferings and pierced, in places,
admixed with lightning gifts
of jeweled graces.

Words from tears …

not extracted, exactly,
- like shrapnel –
nor drained
- like vegetable water –
but pondered
- not pealed –

more that the essence
of experience shakes down in the telling
coming into words for a while,
like scent, color or even the structure of a flower,
hoping to help the healing:
full of goodness and ripe for sustaining life
- until next time it is touched
and turned into new words.

Words touched by tears ...

picked,
carefully,
off the experience of marriage
like wool-to-be-woven into cloth
to clothe the children through the ever-growing years
- each unique, uniquely unfolding –
drawing on what was written:
seeding futures.

"A Pain-Breaking Word" of Encouragement

As you will know from the experience of life we need others; and, whatever the problems of being with others, we need to be in-relationship to be "real". Therefore, whatever the passage of life we are passing through, look for fellow travelers and travel together - for what you are going through is just as much a word for others as their plight is a word for you; and, in reality, there are so many ways that the times that seemed so cramped in the company of others goes on unfolding in a help beyond times and telling. Whether it is about whether to marry or to follow a different path, whether it is the thorn in the midst of marriage or whether it is the many and various challenges of growing children - there is a sharing which is Christ in our midst with a word to help us to persevere.

Writing this poem began, then, during a weekend away with a few communities of the *Neocatechumenal Way,* as a part of a formation in the Christian Faith for adults, when I had already been told that I had spoken enough; and, alternating between being humbled and hurt I wondered which would prevail and what prayer I needed to pray to roll, as it were, with the punch. Then there was the word of the blind man who called out, repeatedly, even though Christ's disciples told him to be "silent" (Lk 18: 39) and the beautifully bright light of the morning and the illuminated leaves compelling the conviction that the words of a short prayer had suddenly filled with meaning: "Glory be to the Father and to the Son and to the Holy Spirit". In other words a "moment" made sense that giving glory to God is a prayer of thanksgiving for His gifts - beginning with His gift of passing through my impenetrable unbelief and coming to lift me out of a suicidal decline by making it possible for me to believe that God exists to help us! Out of these various thoughts and experiences grew, then, the words of this poem.

A PAIN-BREAKING WORD

Like the rain-wet,
drifting, leafy waves of fallen leaves,
or the light-filled blossoming colors on a trembling tree,
or the sudden, tingling touch of a kiss,
words which were dull suddenly alight with meaning -
giving glory to God for the good He has done:

of being pulled from the suffocating, squelching squeeze of the
collapsed hope that maddens the mind:
the black-holed burying of the living;

of shabbily splendored ways burgeoning from the wintry skeletons
of the stark-black isolating loneliness in the day;

of being pulled from the run of wrecking relationships
and ringed to one wife
instead of the unrestrained straying of a wild dog;

of being blessed beyond the unbearable loss of a child torn from life
with children blossoming through all kinds of difficulties;

of collecting qualifications when the years were an unqualified

chronicle of failing to furnish a future beyond
the repetition of unfinished courses;

of gathering the scattered together,
called to heap the coals alight,
and letting the gentle breeze kindle the warmth of company;

of writing through the useless years to the ripe-times for words
which recognize death's tasted passing in illnesses and pain
being out-shone by life's blazing burning of dead experience
in the seasoning of sufferings sanctified through the Word of God.

FAILURE'S FOG

I began this piece out of the very consciousness of the difficulties of
not getting anywhere, financially, with the goal of earning a living
from writing. As I pondered failure more and more, there was a kind
of axis to the whole piece which turned around a saying by Fr. Ian
Ker, namely, out of the failure of the crucifixion comes the
resurrection – not a resuscitation but a transformation whereby even
the familiar appearance of Christ became unfamiliar and He was not
automatically recognized (cf. Jn 20: 11-18).

FAILURE'S FOG
is subtly solid:
not just a misty conglomeration of what rises from the past
but a more present, tangible, bill-dropping-on-the-mat
reminder of the collapse of financial success

from writing.

But the collapse of writing's rewards
is a complete fiction in that the hoped-for-success
never followed the sending of words
to be published.

Years of income scarcely covers
the price of paper drafts for proof-reading;
and so there is always the background argument
about whether and how it will be possible to continue.

And as the children grow out of our
low income status for statutory support,
so the writer's "providential window" begins to close
and the question of paid employment
returns and returns and returns.

What wonderful imaginings
there have been of amazing book sales
which, like Autumn leaves,
have fallen to become compost,
along with wild expectations of publicity,
acclaim and academic awards,
along with almost any hope of any income
from the multiplication of words.

What writing is possible in view of failure's foreboding

foreclosing of financial stability
is not exactly easy –
the slow finger-freezing futility
rising up like a keyboard rebellion:
a kind of battery failure but not of stored charges
so much as the challenge of fighting off the pointlessness
of pitiless pay.

Prayer
puts me in tension between
giving up and going on:

walking my wife and I steadily
through the dropping-down-days
of faltering, swaying and hard to control steps,
when waiting for replies is as difficult as seeking
elusively slippery and slow to find expressions
for struggling thoughts that barely surface

and writing to the end of the day
is like forming letters out of treacle
and writing on sand.

But the opportunity to write arose out of a failure
to remain where those that had fostered me had already left;
failure, already, was a friend:
it rescued me from the time-absorbing
hours-of-over-time-working-out

how to stay employed.

Failure to earn anything from the first books
challenged me to change how I worked;
and, writing now, I often include a response
from others to what I have written.

Writing my way into a more popular style
has, literally, been rewarded by a
neighbor's exclamation
that it helped her with her mother's grief
encouraging me,
against the fading hope of a fortune,
to write again about the reality of life.

Advertising time has arisen from a startling sentence
to an almost full-time invention of words of appeal
peopling the imagination with invitations
to read, to buy and to review,
only to bring the fresh fear of
nothing left to say except
to write about reading
what is written.

Advertising was an adversary
turned friend as feedback
informs what is written
to enhance its force.

But writing is not just a living
but the very breathing
of being a writer
and even if,
in asphyxiating times,
it is difficult to write,

when work is work
times work,

like gasping for pockets of air
in a sinking ship
that keeps hope alive
for another day's
words.

But
just as the crucifixion of Jesus Christ
was a cosmic failure
fruiting the resurrection,
so failure's fog
is a blindness
to its benefits.

Let us actively wait
on the God of action
who waits for the right moment
to act out of love for us.

CLOTS

Like rubbish in a stream, litter on a beach or glass in the park, little by little it accumulates and, if the passer-by is as careless as the original dropper, so it increases exponentially – as if going unnoticed is a license to its multiplication and expansion: to its dropping and the neglect of its collecting until it has spread across the landscape like the remains of scavengers. Culture-junk can gather in the same way, somehow attracting attention to itself and sticking in the newspaper, on the highway or in a gallery; and, afterwards, there is a kind of emptiness where once there was a space: a dereliction of usefulness, of beauty or of a place to be and to gather.

The following piece was written out of the angst that arose after Christmas, when the end of last year had been about advertising what was written rather than about writing a fresh rush of words; the holiday had its upsets and illnesses, as well as gathering us for family games, visits, outings, clearing up and generally withdrawing from writing. So as the time to write returned, so the fear grew of having nothing to say than that of "buy the book and review it"; and, it was while thinking about this that the comparison emerged with blood clotting and, ironically, the start of another poem.

In all, however, it seems that the process of writing a poem is more difficult than writing the prose to go with it; and, therefore, maybe this is a part of the different activity involved in each. In the case of poems, it is more like synthesizing a thread of experience; whereas, in the case of the prose, it is about referring to the fabric from which it came.

CLOTS

grow quietly,

collecting in the veins

like hoover dust:

a matted mixture of bits,

disappointments,

almost twigs of pen lids and pencils,

like beaver dams,

– ending up a dense clogging

visible to ultrasound's

soundless seeing.

Months

of advertising

published writing

has grown the fear of a

writing clot:

of constantly thinking

of a simpler way of adverting

to the already written work

is a service of selling

the words already written –

but it gnaws at writing about

the universe and our relationships

and releases advertising plans

in the place of writing projects

which,

like debris,

threaten to cloggle the imagination
with the inescapable toil of asking
a reader to buy a book and review it,
the possibility of retirement
and muddled, muddy worries about
working elsewhere.

While clotting has a place in nature,
as advertising contributes to the culture of work,
both excessive clotting and an overactive
preoccupation with selling

steals the time needed to ponder
the way words work through the
structure of experience and share,
mysteriously,
in the being of what exists:
as if words,
or what makes words,
begins to make being transparent
even if, like ourselves, there is always
a depth of articulation and explanation
beckoning beyond when last it was
plumbed,

ending and pointing into
the interiority of being.

When clotting,
however,
becomes life-threatening
there are doctors and medicines –
when a writer slows to the point of dribbling words –
and reconsidering reworking and rehashing
what was once exciting is almost all consuming
then what will strip back to the writing
running between being and me?

What will thrill through the writer anew,
thumping and trembling,
thought-struggling
to say what is striven for as clearly as possible
but, like the newly wed, with
that wondrous leisure of love's
discovering what is to be discovered?

What sources will run again when what ran runs dry?

The ever-opened sources of the Word,
the world and human experience.

Praying through the difficulties
raises a surprising turn to talk

of clotting:

a kind of opening on reality
that reads right into the problem,
prodding, like a prospector, for
a seam to stream again like light
bursting through a crack
in an opening door:

of beginning again.

GAPS

Maybe "Gaps" applies more to prose than to poetry – but perhaps it depends on how well a particular type of writing is known.

In general, each of us carries an expressibility that turns on our very individuality and is in every way about the uniqueness of our perception; and, in its way, this will vary according to that awareness of what we experience and the challenges of communicating it. There are those who exploit novelty and will write, almost, in any way that disrupts a convention, from writing nothing to writing down everything; and, indeed, just as with any type of creativity, there are those who draw on its depths and innovate, as it were, through the necessity of expression. Thus there is a sense in which people naturally complement one another in all kinds of ways, whether as writers, artists, sculptors, scientists or musicians; but then also, within each kind of work or indeed across several, variations continue to multiply and generate styles and movements.

But then there is an everyday way in which we speak with each other and notice a daffodil growing on the windowsill, with the light showing through an envelope at the end of the green shoot, housing the emergence of the yellow flower head, or a daughter coming back from the paper round long after her brother because she was reading the news and saw a house without steps and went back to photograph it or another who knows what films have been released, what authors are about, what gadgets exist, what ways sportsmen and women train. In other words there is a kind of endlessness to what different people will notice and comment on and investigate – bringing bits and pieces of what they have found to the conversation.

Then there are those deeper dynamics which are to do with a truth, like the beginning of a human being and the extent to which this has been understood and the open-ended questions that still remain to be answered. When there is, as in the case of understanding human conception, so many voices which contribute to this dialogue it takes time for a specific question to emerge and to be answered. Thus, little by little, possibly over many years, there is a search-gathering of many kinds of contributions to the question and the seeing, maybe from early on, that there is an exciting trail to be followed, old and new paths, turning in ways that begin to draw different enquiries together. "Gaps", ultimately, then, is about that journeying through the world of research which begins to "twitch", like the hawthorn twig, in the presence of flowing answers; and, while being jealous of an idea or a discovery begins to bring about the desire to hide an insight, the prevailing desire to communicate and to be in contact and to publish wins over the flight from publishing and the fear of it being stolen.

GAPS

are spaces between objects:
planets and particles,
positive and negative,
generating movement,
channeling energy,
engaging the dynamic difference
between us:

a gap is not without shape,
like the missing piece of a puzzle
but not so simply defined:

a "place" where the perception of others
comes together, like the spectrum of colors, flashing white
illuminating more of the whole than a single eye
could ever encompass:

not random rays colliding and bouncing
off edges and planes but an orchestrated
gathering of what belongs together.

So just as many leaves, vegetable remains and rotting fruits
just as soil and compost and seeds
just as sun and rain and frosts

generate the dynamic conditions of plant life

so gathering what we can of the thoughts of others

helps us to see the gaps that get us going

on the research which bends the years

like the path of star-light

around the sun

as our subject

absorbs

us more

and more

until,

like the critical mass,

of source upon source

witnesses the presence of a really

unanswered question

and writing upon writing

to the dialogue driven

by the gaps between us

to follow the pointers homing

in on a newly observed discovery:

that our existence is not a theory,

a possibility

but a fact

from the

beginning.

Soundings

If "Gaps" is not about market research – although *markets* there need to be and *research* is always one of the necessary starting points – then "Soundings" is not so much about determining whether or not a book is going to be written as how it is going to come together. Indeed, there are probably many ways that a structure can emerge from the material, either because there is a common denominator, like Scripture[1], which brings it all together or because, having begun and persevered through the uncertainties of where it is going, the question of the axis on which it turns, by which to include this and exclude that, is always present and, in a way, can result in a single work turning into a trilogy[2].

Alternatively, while the seed of a book can come from elsewhere, like a circular requesting an article on a certain subject and, as it was pondered, so the author realized that he had enough material for his own book[3]. Nevertheless, each particular book has to develop, and so it is the very fact that development takes place that encourages the writer; and, in addition, encourages the writer to engage with other writers for its enrichment, which again emerges as an indicator that there is a real thread to be unravelled, a territory to be navigated or a mosaic to be laid.

---

[1] Hence the first book that was published was called *Scripture: A Unique Word*, Cambridge Scholars Publishing, 2014.

[2] This was the case with the development of the trilogy on faith and reason called: *From Truth and truth*, all three of which were published by Cambridge Scholars Publishing.

[3] This happened with *Mary and Bioethics: An Exploration* – forthcoming from En Route Books and Media, 2020.

But thinking about it further may be "Soundings" is more about the meaningfulness of the work itself. Indeed, a kind of varied range of "feedback" is certainly about research and the structuring of the work – but perhaps the emphasis of this particular piece is about determining whether or not it is true, worthwhile and even deep enough to go on with.

SOUNDINGS
begin
without a book
being complete
and writing it
is a search-sounding:

different starting points,
starting differently,
until the whole
comes into view,

like grasping
the intersection
of colored lights,

an end
to the beginning
in the beginning
that begets the end.

Wherefrom
returns the sound
of our sounding?

Is it from the echo
in the universe of the
movements we make,
returning to us,
finally,

rebounding down the molecules
in the air to the very
highway of the nerve from
our ear to our brain –
as if we are but conductors
without communication:
a kind of terminal of transmissions?

Or is it that there is feedback from
the evidence which returns from our probing
and redoubles or trebles the pitch of our enquiry:
raising question after question in the dialogue
between what exists and ourselves,

since we are never as alone as we think,

engaging us in a kind of dialogical wrestling
as we endeavor to disentangle all the conflicting

claims about the imposition of meaning,
meaninglessness and the inherent meaning
of what actually exists
being what we are really
discovering?

Or is it that there are
sounds which emerge in the silence
and altogether speak of a submerged word:

a word within the world,
sounding still,

reverberating as it was once spoken
but in a way as if it is still speaking;
and, therefore, sounding

is a kind of prayerful searching
into what originates in the depths
of being:

a kind of exchange between our existence
and the still-dynamism of the dynamic stillness
which sings a melody in reach of listening
if only we are tuning in to hear it?

But then there is that expressed word,
that biblical articulation of common experience

in language both difficult and accessible

that resounds between us and itself,

suggesting truths to be told and

helps to be had

if we uncover

the silting up of what once

ran freely between us

and God:

the Word of Life.

Soundings

are not separate,

discreet, unrelated responses;

they fit,

like strands of a rope,

strengthening the purpose

and even pulling

the work apart in order

to bring together

its final shape.

MATTER

The "pathetic fallacy" is a literary expression that refers to the world, often the weather, being an expression of the mood or characteristics of a character in a story. But, deeper than that, the outward nature of the universe can "echo" the inward nature of the human person. In other words, it is not just that a writer can "devise" a weather mood to indicate the plight or mentality of a people it is, rather, that the very universe stands to be drawn upon to express the nature of human being; and, therefore, the potential of the universe to express the inner life of the human being is evidence that there is a profound coherence between both the universe as a whole and its potential to express human experience. In other words the coherence that exists between the potential of the "outward" universe as a whole, and every detail of it, *to express the interiority of the human person* is a coherence that goes beyond coincidence to the same extent that understanding events as providential goes beyond seeing every encounter as about as significant as the roll of a dice.

"Matter", then, is about that common use of imagery and ideas which, in itself, goes beyond just being an indifferent fact of our lived in-universe-experience.

MATTER

is elastic,

pulls apart and reshapes,

like water forming spheres

of sprinkled beads on a shiny surface,

and dissolving into a pool and flowing,

as if energized like molten silver when,

sparklingly bright

they run together

and trickle down

to the ground.

Particles, pulled apart,
form other particles,
as if there is never nothing
but always something,

however small and short-lived,
like libraries, books, chapters, sections
and sub-sections, paragraphs
words and letters.

Words can be shaken down into letters,
lying inert, in potential to be written again,
again and again, into other words;
writing is a work

like dry-stone walling:

of word upon word
being used without dropping it back to the ground
but always being placed, if possible, in the sentence,
carrying the communication on,
not dividing space
but uniting people.

Words,
can be difficult, too,
and themes, like seams in the rock,
while worth the time and effort

are sometimes exceedingly slow to extricate
and are more like the cutting of blocks
with which to build
than the use of what is found.

But the flow,
like the running of pebbles,
can pour down and make a surround,
setting off the difficulties
like a jewel in its setting.

Matter,
snapping into shape,
is always something,

and, in the same way,
words are almost impossible
to use meaninglessly – but

may my words
always be
load
bearing.

GUEST POET AND POEM: DR. MARY ANNE URLAKIS

Mary Anne Urlakis is a classically lettered American Bioethicist, staunchly devoted to defending the sanctity of every human life from the moment of fertilization to natural death. She holds three graduate degrees in Philosophy and Bioethics and is currently pursuing a second doctorate in Theology. Dr. Urlakis is a writer, speaker, Catholic radio show host, photographer, and poet. Dr. Urlakis has been married for 30 years and treasures her vocation as wife and the mother of ten children- eight living- as the most cherished of her roles. Much of her work is inspired by the manifestation of the goodness of God revealed through the transcendentals in the mundane moments of everyday life.

The Empty Lot: Three photographs by Joseph Urlakis to accompany his mother's poem; and, indeed, as each picture brings to the fore more of what is "there" so, it seems, the pictures imitate the art of pondering what there is to see.

"The Empty Lot":
An Introduction by the author, Dr. Mary Anne Urlakis.

The passage: "So shall my word be that goes forth from my mouth, it shall not return to me empty, but shall do what pleases me, achieving the end for which I sent it (Isaiah 55:11)," inspired me to write The Empty Lot. The poem is allegorical and reflects both the nature of the soul of the writer as well the transcendental reality of the world around us.

As poets and writers we are challenged with the task of capturing truths- some of which are self-evident, and some of which are nuanced- and presenting them to an audience in a manner that resonates with individual and collective personal experience while simultaneously sparking wonder and awe. We are often like children collecting fireflies in a jar in the twilight of a warm Summer eve. Our targets are moving and elusive, yet when captured together they unite to emit a luminous delight.

When we examine the human condition, our own lives, families, and vocations, there is a temptation to focus on that which superficially appears empty or has been labeled as a failure. In prayer, when we choose to offer our past, present, and future fully to the loving God Who fashioned our inmost being, and Who invites us each day to embrace the life He alone created us to live, we find the grace to appreciate the profound beauty of the mystery of our existence. In so doing, we become cognizant that the Divine Logos by Whom we were created, through Whom we live and move and have our being, and to Whom we are ultimately called to live in eternal ineffable communion, is ever active in achieving the end for which He is sent.

As writers our empty lot is often an empty page. As human persons, our empty lot is the horizon of life and eternity which unfolds before us. Each has its share of thorns and briars, yet each also holds the secret of eternal beauty waiting to be revealed.

THE EMPTY LOT

To some who pass by
The empty lot
Is an over-grown tangle of weeds
A waste of space
A void of nothingness
An economic failure.

To some who ponder
The empty lot

It holds the secrets of a history
The memories of past years lie hidden,
Sheltered beneath the tall grass
Where rabbits and field mice nest with their young
And the circle of life inexorably spins.

To some who delight in the rustic beauty of
The empty lot
It is pregnant with possibility.
The sweet fragrance of wildflowers pulses through the breeze
As a white-speckled fawn steadies itself to nurse from a young doe-
mother.
Poetry written by the Divine Hand manifests to the soul who is still
And receptive to drink in the abundant beauty freely given by He
Who waits with love to share the gift of His Creation.

Part VII: After

Just as "Before" points to beginnings so "After" points to endings; but just as a beginning is also a change from not-beginning or even non-existence so an end is also a change from temporal to eternal time; and just as temporal time is only and ever present, even as it changes, so eternal time is only and ever in the present.

This final section, then, also functions as a kind of note board of further thoughts; but, however, we are entering the field of speculation about the nature of the very end of time – whether that end is individual or communal. Even an individual death, however, has a bearing on the community of which he or she is a part; and, as regards the final end of all things, it will no doubt be different for each of us even if it happens, simultaneously, for all who are alive at that moment of the very end of time as we know it.

What follows, then, is not so much an eschatology, an account of the end times, as notes towards thinking through the fact that just as there are beginnings there are also endings; but just as there are beginnings and endings so there are pivotal moments of change. There are changes which take us into, through or from the changes of time: dying itself; the agony of dying as an irreversible, irrevocable and life-giving grace of giving-back the gift of life; dying, almost as in dying back, the gift of life broken out of our grip; and, finally, that tide of experiences which take us to the edge and back, that tempt us to retreat from the changes to which we are constantly called.

Having said that, however, there is an influence of Newman that I want to make explicit:

"At present we are in a world of shadows. What we see is not substantial. Suddenly it will be rent in twain and vanish away, and our maker will appear. And then, I say, that first appearance will be nothing less than a personal intercourse between the Creator and every creature. He will look on us, while we look on Him"[1].

Thus there are threads and influences from Newman's thought and work which, together with reflections of my own, contribute to the view that "Heaven would be hell to an irreligious man", for "if we wished to imagine a punishment for an unholy, reprobate soul, we perhaps could not fancy a greater than to *summon it to heaven*"[2]. In other words what this communicates is the purpose of love: that God's love is Love's longing for us to come into His presence and to rejoice; however, if we reject the company of the One who wants to be with us, we are living an excruciating experience of refusing to drink at the fountain of life and yet we are abysmally thirsty. Just as being away from my wife and children filled me with a terrible longing to be with them, and yet it was frustrated by delays which intensified it, so imagine an everlasting frustration of the fulfilment of the very longing

---

[1] Cited by Fr. Ian Ker, in his book called *Healing The Wound of Humanity: The Spirituality of John Henry Newman*, London: Darton, Longman and Todd, 1993, on p. 106, from *Parochial and Plain Sermons*, 8 vols: *PS* v. 3-4.

[2] Cited by Fr. Ian Ker, in his book called *Healing The Wound of Humanity*, p. 106, *PS* i. 5-7.

that would fill us with an eternal happiness.

THREE TIMES – NOW A FOURTH, FIFTH AND SIXTH

Trilogies, in a way, are opportunities to visit a subject a number of times, to reflect a closer relationship between pieces of work or to recognize, even after the fact, that there is a structure to thought that goes beyond our individual acts of thinking and writing; indeed, it is almost as if there is a compass that is constantly structuring our travel through different terrains so that, in passing, we can see the landscape more completely by taking different vantage points.

So it is, then, with the theme of dying and its possibilities, as when we imagine the flight of the soul through the universe or we are suspended between the onset of death and it being unknown whether or not we will actually die and then, of course, there is visiting as life leaves us and our roots loosen before, finally, there is the reality of death – both for those who have died and for those of us who remain.

But now there is a fifth, too: that bearing of burdens that breaks our grip on life and turns us against it. We need, always, to be at peace about the person who has died and, bearing in mind the widespread cries that burst upon us, perhaps unprepared, it is essential to remember that the mercy of God extends to the depths of a person's passing in ways that we will never understand but can imagine, dimly, like daylight revealing the details of what is visible unlike any other kind of illumination. Thus God can pass in the moment of passing in a way that rescues the most impossible situation; and, if for no other reason, we can only hope that the prayer that rises in us is an outward sign of the grace that came to those who were loved – even as they died, overwhelmed, as in the flooding of the difficulties of life.

Finally, there is that untimely dying, a child torn from life through the tragedy that grew within and showed, unfortunately, too abruptly to be helped.

Thus this is now a quartet plus two: Part I: Dying; Part II: The Plight of All; Part III (I): Visiting; Part III (II): The Plight of Passing; Part IV: He was Among Us; and, finally, Part V: One Life Uprooted.

PART I: DYING

Admitting thoughts about death can be very embarrassing as, I recall, there was a time when I went through a long period of loneliness and, it seemed, it was almost as if life was passing like a slow bleed; and, without a lot of experience of love, or friendship, but rather many kinds of crises and dead-ends, there was some kind of background idea that sprang from somewhere that it would be a loss to die without having lived the love of a woman.

Then there are those times when it almost seems as if there is a desire to die, like walking down the middle of a road, almost willing to have an accident and hoping against hope that I would not die; as, in that time, there seemed to be no end to the questions and difficulties of life and going on was almost as impossible as bringing it all to an end. There are those who go out at night in black, on a black evening, particularly black if it's cloudy and wet and who, narrowly missed by cars or who slip by on bikes, risk collision, maiming or death.

Losing a child was indescribably painful and I have written about it directly in previous books, and indirectly in this one, a loss that almost never heals although it fades, at times, until it is more fully remembered again and brings me to tears and prayer. Then, awhile later, there was the sudden death of my father, a kind of losing the wall around the childhood garden and feeling, almost frighteningly, the cold winds blowing through the garden; and, also, a renewed prayer for him and a regretful remembering of what an unwilling son I had been – all too ready to run off and play football instead of help dad with the alterations in the house that he wanted to make. So when he was taking down the wall between a dining room and a pantry all I wanted to do was to get out and play: a different kind of dying in the relationship of son to father. The death of my mother was more difficult in a different way as she died of cancer and her death was a step-by-step decline over several months but very noticeably a deterioration into almost total inactivity; and, therefore, from being very active and smiling she became practically unable to move and even to breathe and sitting with her entailed singing psalms, quietly, as I shared her suffering. It was comforting to discover, too, that hearing is one of the last things to go.

So when my own illnesses started to come with clotting on the leg and lungs, pneumonia and pleurisy, all at once, having married and now having two young children with a third on the way, lying in a hospital bed was a blessed relief from the effort to work, to put the bin out, to write or to relate to my wife and children. Thoughts of death, then, were more about looking forward to a rest and, at the same time, wondering about the lives I might be leaving behind. At other times, as the children grew older, so I wondered about whether I would see them into life – but even then the thought of praying for them here and hereafter seemed to subtly undo the difference between being alive and dead. Then as other illnesses came and went and the death of other people, too, and the years passed with so many more than expected, the family growing to eight children, with two more in heaven, my imagined death took a different turn and led to what I have written below – not so much from the point of view of the uprooting pain unleashed in losing others as the possibility of glimpsing, however briefly, the amazing scope of the universe as I "leave" it.

DYING

is wilting to the point of loosening roots being freed
from the experience of a lived life –

and leaving is very different
from being left behind.

Dying is rising, pulling away,
parting and passing upon prayers
to the hidden Helper visible to the opening eye,

wholly given without being wholly asked,
but asking increases the gift and makes present,

faster than light, brighter than white,
the goal of God driven by prayer.

Together we dwell within and through
the structure of atoms,
exploring the multi-shaped
mesh of molecules and their surfaces:

arising out of pulsing parts
clouding and colliding in gases
sliding and slipping in liquids
arrested when frozen
and relatively fixed when solid
but all, equally, extraordinarily
translucent energies.

Colored or colorless in passing,
depending on gliding close
or winging through the intricate interiors
diving upwards and outwards into the
deepest reaches of the sea amidst the brightnesses
the startling beauties in the black dark,
bubbly broken with almost neon
blips of incandescent blops of light
strangely visible and visibly strange.

On and into the sky light blue
skimming the clouds, ascending the steep white cliffs,
climbing the rain, whirling through the winds,
racing birds, jumping up upon up-drafts
and running upon light beams
as if drawing into the welter of plasma
is a beckoning beholding of splashing
and crashing of energy.

Rushing and soaring into space,

traversing immeasurable distances,
delighting in the misty, mixed, patching
of objects and dust, stars and planets
and downing into a black hole
irresistibly silent, solidifying atoms.

Dying is diving,
together, imperceptibly separating, yet at once,
if touching is impossibly possibly possible,
if arriving it can be called,
in the intense brilliance

of the Presence of Being
surrounded through and through
or translating from place to place
if position existed for the multitude of transfigured
creatures in the mystery
of creation-in-God[3].

PART II: THE PLIGHT OF ALL

Gordon Nary wrote to me a while ago and surprised me with an invitation to be interviewed for his website, *Profiles in Catholicism*[4]

---

[3] Again, but more remote influence of Newman, probably from the *Dream of Gerontius.*

[4] Go to: https://www.catholicprofiles.org/post/april-15-2020-profiles-in-catholicism; and cf., https://www.catholicprofiles.org/post/an-interview-with-francis-etheredge.

and, in due course, I commented on the fact that as he was getting older he needed to make provision for the continuation of his work; and, therefore, whether we approach death through the timeliness of a long life or whether, as in a whole variety of ways, it comes through accidents, illness or tragedies, it is a subject which impacts us all.

In this time, then, of the outbreak of the coronavirus and our subsequent, almost universal lockdown, he has invited me to write a number of prayers in view of different situations; and so, beginning with "The Plight of All", there is the fact that our Prime Minister, Boris Johnson, has not only been hospitalised but has also been taken into intensive care too. Moreover, while the number of people taken ill, dying or dead, varies across the world, the agony that it involves for each person and family is equally acute and its turmoil intense. Therefore, while I read about Boris Johnson[5] in order to write this prayer, I also wanted to write it in such a way that it opens upon the suffering we have in common and which, in one way or another, has drawn close to many of us at this time.

At the same time, however, let us acknowledge that there are times when public service entails a risk, in a variety of ways, for healthcare workers, emergency rescuers, the police, the military and indeed for anyone going to the help of others. Therefore, while all of us are in front of death and dying at particular times, and sometimes more than once, let us remember those who are, for whatever reason, close to it at this particular time.

---

[5] Cf. https://en.wikipedia.org/wiki/Boris_Johnson.

THE PLIGHT OF ALL

Father

You alone
Know the heart
Of each one of us:

The time to live and the time to die
Is a time we scarcely recognize

But come it will,
Either alone or in company,
Easing our passage
Or filling it with pain.

Take pity on our lives
Lived recklessly or not,
Flamboyantly or discreetly,
Publicly or in our street.

An angel companion beside us,
Addressing our lives in reality,
Preparing us for eternity.

Whether we live or die,
Serve in public or our neighbour,
We live amidst so many others,

Weeping or worse.

Help us in the breach of passing,
To leave love's touch
On the hearts from whom
We're drawn

– suspended –

As if in the hands of a Gardener,
Deciding whether to transplant
Us to eternity or to delay awhile.

Pity us and those we love!
Love those we love imperfectly!
Repair and rebuild what is broken!
Forgive and prepare us to live!

Or let us pass,
Prepared,
Patiently,
From here
To you.

And let Your love
Enfold the left
As leaving,
We leave in the hope

Of love enfolding
Each of us.

Mother Mary,
Meet us in the doorway,
Greet us or ask
Your Son for the
Pardon or the pause
Which completes
The gift of life
We have been given.

PART III (1): VISITING

In this next prayer-poem, again requested by Gordon Nary, we remember people who are in nursing homes and, indeed, those who are caring for them, whether cooking, washing dishes, cleaning, nursing, doctors-on-call, fundraising or otherwise helping with occasional crafts, entertainments and outings; and, even if all are not mentioned, yet the implication of their presence is still there as well as the many who, under normal circumstances, are able to visit, whether related to residents or not.

But there are many other situations where people are often, but not always limited in their movements, particularly refugees who are suffering, in addition to all the other difficulties they are experiencing, the further problems of being part of a large number of people confined to a particular area. What kinds of problems there are, are certainly compounded by the fact that those who are organizing their welfare are also having to take measures to ensure that neither the refugees nor those caring for them are likely to pass on illnesses to those around them. Indeed, is it possible to hope against hope that people are able to find ingenious ways of helping each other in these unusual circumstances?

Equally poignant, perhaps, are those imprisoned who, for whatever crime, are so close to one another as to make it difficult to provide for the health of prisoners, the staff, and all who visit; and, therefore, there could be an exponential increase in isolation, not because of security measures, but because of securing the health of everybody.

Aside, however, from those in nursing homes, designated camps and prisoners are the large numbers of people who have had to leave the cities in view of the loss of work, income and accommodation. Whatever the condition of the home villages or towns from which many of these people have come the sheer, sudden increase of numbers is going to add additional strains to many communities.

There are, then, many situations in which visiting is a simple, even essential form of solidarity with others and which, in this present time, is difficult if not impossible to facilitate easily; and, given the social expression of the nature of human being, visiting could even be considered to be a basic human right.

Let us pray for them all!

A particular prayer for those with the coronavirus in nursing homes – but remember the needs of others too:

Visiting

Oh Father, it is true we no longer visit those in care
But we remember those we know who are there:
Whether once a nurse, a writer, a mother
A teacher, a priest, a doctor-social-activist
Members of a circus now using the zimmer
When once they flew and leapt and danced,
And those unknown but known to you who
Sleep, or weep or go about quietly, pausing,
Forgetting, going back to and forth –

And we beg you to be with each of them;

Oh Father, it is true our children no longer visit
But we share the memory of coming and going
Of running to and fro and finding the people we knew
Of avoiding bumping and bouncing into others
And taking a picture-card, telling news or simply
Listening, talking, as children do, about this and that
And learning of very different times and lives
Whether here, there or elsewhere or further away
Of interests sometimes past or wholly present –

And we beg each guardian angel to be vigilant;

Oh Father, it is true we do not know when we can go again
And sometimes we pass where once we could call

Recognizing the entrance and the difficulties within
Imagining the struggles to help and heal as weaker
We know, each one grows with the passing of time
And those once so free to roam now resting,
Possibly, before their final parting and last breath
Hopefully comfortable, ready to leave, to fly
Even if unplanned and at an unexpected time to leave –

And we beg the saints to remember them.

Oh Lord, Jesus Christ, I often fell asleep when I went
Or drifted to the television and joined in the silence
Wishing to be elsewhere, talking to someone else
Or leaving before the time to sing the song
Before meals that embarrassed us but was a blessing
To those who listened, smiled and clapped –

Forgive us and renew our going out to others again
Whether old and young together, educating each other,
Sharing lives and experience, helping in being helped
And helping in being able to help another;

Oh Lord, Jesus Christ, our children sat alone and ate the biscuits
Or skipped too soon to roll down the sloping grass
Or sat in clumps beyond the full but quiet rooms
Or chatted to each other, behind a chair, sneaking out,
Or took a book and read instead of reading to others
Or were absorbed in the scrolling screens –

Forgive us and rouse us to see the needs of others
Whether known to us or too far from those who know them,
Or abandoned, neglected or overlooked in the busy times
Of day that need the simple grace of being noticed now;

Oh Lord, we had our favorites and failed to talk with many,
Sat alone and reluctantly stirred, were slow to see
Those without visits, rocking or repeating questions,
Statements, gestures, worries, or troubles, whether
Recent or remote and let slip many moments between
Words and observations and ways of starting up again –

Forgive us and help us to find you in the presence of others
Whether rich or poor, worn out or bright, or sitting in the long
Silence of slowly subsiding, crumbling minds, alive and lonely
In the isolation of being hidden in the routines of the day.
Oh Holy Spirit, Lord of Life and Love, pass among us,
And multiply the many acts of human kindness that
Are fruits of Jesus Christ, delighting the Father, adorning
The day like spring-fresh buds and the blooming of flowers;

Oh Holy Spirit, Lord of Life and Love, pass among us,
Reconciling us to one another, to our families, to the life
We have lived and the love poured out, wisely or not,
Raising a blessing, like a sunset unveiling gold from heaven;

Oh Holy Spirit, Lord of Life and Love, pass among us,
Inspiring new ways to help us with all the challenges

Of illness, care, finding cures and managing today,
Refreshing old investigations and breaking new ground;

Oh Holy Spirit, Lord of Life and Love, pass among us,
Renew again the vocation to serve, going beyond our fears
To the many verges of the world, whether near or far,
Giving life to dried out hearts and deserted lives;

Oh Holy Spirit, Lord of Life and Love, pass among us,
With Jesus Christ, His Holy Mother and innumerable
Disciples and witnesses, gathering the gifts of praise,
Lifting our hearts heavenward, helping us into the company of

God the Father the Almighty, Creator of heaven and earth.

Amen[6].

Part III (ii): The Plight of Passing

This third piece on the theme of dying, but now entailing death, was again written in response to a request from Gordon Nary; and, as the request was for a prayer for those who have died from the coronavirus, it was again a matter of thinking concretely of the particular difficulties of this situation but of not neglecting, either, the wider range of what is possible – even if it does not detail the many untold tragedies of life.

---

[6] "Visiting", published in: https://www.catholicprofiles.org/post/june-1-2020-profiles-in-catholicism.

In a certain sense we do die alone, even if we are surrounded by others and indeed they are praying for us; but, too, in this present climate there is often the problem of being unable even to accompany the dying with company and prayers. Thus, in this present situation, it may well be that for some there is an intensification of the suffering of dying as, while hearing lasts, it is difficult to make it possible for anyone to be there. I remember in the case of my mother's death, having been up with her until late I went home to see my wife and children and, in the morning, returned a moment too late to be there for her passing; and, for a long time, I was unable to accept that I had not been there for her death – but, actually, two of my sisters were there and they had read the psalms to her in her last moments. At the same time, though, there are probably many occasions when it is not possible for a relative or friend to be present at the time of death; and, therefore, in many situations of life this experience of dying in a kind of isolation may very well be there – from the most tragic type of death to the most ordinary sleeping the sleep of death.

I have written, then, in such a way as that I hope this account may speak to many who, for one reason or another, at one time or another, it was not possible to be present at the death of one who was loved.

THE PLIGHT OF PASSING

Oh God the Father,
Son and Holy Spirit,
Mary, Mother of the Lord
And all angels and saints:

You are the radiant welcome:
The abundantly beautiful company
Of all who have died – no more alone
Than particles in the plasma of the sun.

Let the grace of passing be as water running clear in your hands,
Our lives as colorful as stones in purest spring water,
Let the grace of passing be as light in the windows of the soul,
Our lives having lost their darkness dripping with brightness,
Let the grace of passing be as spring blossoms, brightly lit flowers,
Our lives as tulips brimming with your luminous presence!

Let your work of redemption not forget the forgotten
And cure the ills of the heart unaddressed in passing
Turning the hopeless to hope and the anguished to peace.

Let your love fill the lives of the left and discover, a-new,
A prayer in the pain of loss and the grief of going
And grant relief to the burdened by cares and worry.

Father – Forgive us:

We could not visit because of isolation
We could not visit for fear of troubling others
We could not help who helped instead of us

We could not be there because of frailty
We could not be there because of distance

We could not be there because of cost

We could not be there because of the living
We could not be there because of the dying
We could not be there because …

Father: Have mercy on us!

Let this long Sunday resound with hope,
And leap as a flame from the fire:
Of Good Friday's suffering;
Holy Saturday's peaceful pause;
And Easter's transfigured rising!
Let this Eastertide be turned into blessings!
Let this time of pain be pierced with Love!

But if any dead lie neglected and any left unloved

Let an angel visit in the moment of need
Healing, tenderly, the wounds still bleeding,
And embrace, with an unbelievable blessing,

The heart broken and the life lived almost lost!

Oh Blessed Trinity in One!
Oh Holy Family!
Oh Witnesses of Love!

Let us beg you
To wake with a welcome
All who have died
And help all who are left!

PART IV: HE WAS AMONG US

As I have already said in my introduction to this growing group of poems, plus one on dying and death, I have written elsewhere of my own attempted suicide[7] and certainly acknowledged, even in this book, the recurrent temptation that comes dressed in one kind of acceptable disguise or another. On the one hand, then, there is the objective truth that our lives are a gift and not ours to end; and, indeed, as my life shows, even after many years of suffering these temptations to end it all, the Lord's word continues to prevail: "I have come so that you may have life and life to the full" (Jn. 10: 10).

Just as with my experience, so too when I have been told of a person's suicide, there is often a sense of untold, and perhaps untellable isolation that often seems to be a part of the circumstances of his or her death; indeed, it is not as if there was not company, family or other people in that person's life – such the death was unexpected, even confounding and confusing given how recently others had been there. Although, perhaps, here and there was a bare glimpse of the possibility that, being so slight, slipped out of sight; but, even in view of the presence of other people, there is a kind of hidden pit, whether trap-door covered or concealed in some other way, that

---

[7] Cf. *The Prayerful Kiss*, 2019, pp. 57-58:
https://enroutebooksandmedia.com/theprayerfulkiss/.

suddenly gives: that opens on an unbearable moment. There may not be a single, identical situation, event or reaction that sits, un-sprung, like an undiscovered wound but which, in time, saps the willingness to live and drains the heart's resistance to a sudden departure; but, nevertheless, there may well be a withering of the will to live by some secret frostbite that, in whatever way, undermines the experience of being loved and the love of life.

Nevertheless, there can open in the hearts of those around the person who died a surprising hope that, just as the person was loved, maybe that love is a life-line even now to the person who has died; and, just as surely as we pray for everyone we know, maybe in the moment of death there is a hopelessness that almost, but not quite, seeks to quench the hope of happiness. So, in the moment of death, there is a thread of gold: the prayer of love: that passes between the living and the dead and forms, hopefully, a net by which to raise the fallen to the feet of Christ.

This prayer is not only for the personal anguish which rises up in our lives but for the many and terrible situations – whether because of war, in war or because of the many other ways that we are afflicted by our fallenness – and for all in whom the depth charges blast, unseen, the heart's hope and silence a life which still needed to un-bear the burdensomeness of untold sufferings.

This prayer, then, requested by Gordon Nary for Corporal Rory Hamill[8], raises again the theme of love's ever hoping against hope for the person loved; and, by extension, for the person who never knew,

---

[8] Go to: "A prayer for Corporal Rory Hamill: He was Among Us": https://www.catholicprofiles.org/post/may-15-2020-profiles-in-catholicism.

had forgotten or failed to discover that Christ's merciful outstretched hand may reach even here, with His merciful touch, where it unbearably hurts un-healed.

HE WAS AMONG US
Almighty God and Father:

He was among us
Then he went ahead
And others were spared
The losses he suffered,
the losses he shared
with others who suffered.

Father, Creator of Heaven and Earth:

How many are lost in war!
How many are lost, embattled, afterwards!
How many are lost in the aftermath of pain:
In the life-long plague of remembering -
The hidden, memorized shock,
Closing, like shrapnel, on the heart!
Father of Our Lord Jesus Christ:

In what dark place are the tears,
In what dark place are the wounds,
In what dark place, darker without you,
Are the questions, questioning you:

Why have I lived?
Why have they died?

Lord God, Son of God:

We were walking together
And he re-joined us
– thank you!
We were walking together
And his stumbling he shared with us
– thank you!
We were walking together
And he helped us
– thank you!

We were walking together
And we lost him
– forgive us!

Lord, True Man and True God:

How many are among
the bushes – sit with us!
How many are alone
on the street – stand with us!
How many are edged
out of life's reach – speak to us!

Lord, through your Death and Resurrection:

May your darkness en-brighten us!
May your sufferings soothe us!
May your words enlighten us!

Oh, Holy Spirit:

Come in the flight upwards
to take the weight downing us!
Come in life's going,
to bring life to the brim in us!
Come in the upset of leaving
to take love to the left!

Oh, Holy Spirit of Love:

Help us to find the openings
for those locked in the past!
Help us to heal the hidden,
Un-yielding wounds!
Help us to end the warring
within each of us
that breaks out between us!

Oh, Holy Spirit, Soul of the Church:

Sing in us! Sigh in us! Save us!

Oh, Holy Mary, Mother of God,
St. Joseph and the whole
host of welcoming Saints.

We have a common prayer:

for all of us, here and there, to share,
for the people passing – and past;
for the past that plagues the present:

We pray for peace and an end
to the life-long price of war.

PART V: ONE LIFE UPROOTED

In what is beginning to emerge as a definite type of contribution to this book of a growing number of "Prayer-Poems", largely due to Gordon Nary's requests, the subject of each has a particular poignancy owing to the personal event that is often at the root of it – even if it swells to embrace a variety of nuances that hope to open, inclusively, a more widespread range of human experience. A prayer for Alejandro Ripley, an autistic child thought to have been killed by his mother[9], likewise is rooted in a tragic event of the death of this child; and, as with anyone's death, there is the impact of the person's absence and,

---

[9]   Cf.   https://edition.cnn.com/2020/05/24/us/alejandro-ripley-killing/index.html; and the poem-prayer is now published in Profiles in Catholicism: https://www.catholicprofiles.org/post/june-15-2020-profiles-in-catholicism.

in view of what has happened, all the other elements of pain, anger, incomprehension, pity and mourning.

At the same time, if the death of one person can move us, and Gordon said he cried when he read this piece, then hopefully the tears will run for all the untimely deaths that ring out to God throughout the world and raise a trickle, then a stream, then a river, then a flood of tears appealing to the Lord to send His Holy Spirit to renew the face of the earth.

ONE LIFE UPROOTED

Dear God the Father, Almighty, Creator of Heaven and Earth,
Your love loves each life into being, both fragile and firm,
Each beautiful, both burgeoning but inheriting a blemish,
Just as your love acts in the union out of which we spring,
So you enrich us with the many helps that, together,
Strengthen, color and enhance our gift of life
Swelling, growing, expressing what is hidden –

Receive the sprouting seed, the seedling, the young plant,
Prematurely plucked from the soil that nourished it,
Tragically uprooted, not transplanted, withered not watered.
Dear Lord, Only Son of the Father, Merciful Redeemer of All,
You know the plight of parents, their struggles and strife,
The long hours and lonely difficulties that blight our lives,
You know both the delights and the temptations that would
Turn us back from the beginning that you planned and planted
Between us, as delicate as a fledgling plant, too helpless

To roam far and wide, too young to leave, too needy to be left –

Forgive the suppressing suffocation of the help we did not seek,
The terrible turning from the turn towards you to complete
What you began and wanted to flourish in the fullness of life.

Oh Holy Spirit and Lord of Life, Gift from Gift and Help of All,
Turn us all to the help of each and everyone who lives:
Turn parents back to their children's nurture and neediness,
Turn mother's back from being lost in labyrinthine ways,
Turn father's back to loving their wives and helping in the home,
Turn children back to discovering their good gifts, freely given,
Turn the family back to fostering the good of all.

Dear Jesus, Son of Mary and Child in the Care of St. Joseph,
You lived through the childhood of children,
Silently but significantly present, inviting us to remember
Your presence among us at all times and in any place –

Walk with us through all our joys and sorrows and
Show us, in ways unique to you, how to heal broken wounds
And accompany those untimely taken to the Father's heart;

Dear Mary, Mother of the Lord and Spouse of Joseph,
You passed in the midst of many and profound sufferings,
You know the hardship of fleeing violence, struggling with little,
Opening your home to others and being with your dying son –

Make your presence known to us in the daily difficulties of life,
Bringing consolation, hope and inspiration to pass through
The impassable problems, whether obvious or hidden;

Dear St. Joseph, Guardian of the Child Jesus and Spouse of Mary,
You experienced the trials of poverty and persecution,
Protecting your family and trading in uncertain times,
Opening your skills and talents to those around you –

Lead us in recovering our neglect as husbands and fathers,
Guiding us in our work, recreation and choice of companions,
Enabling us to bridge home and work, faithful to all.

Oh Blessed Trinity, Origin of Creation and all that is good,
Cause of the people of God and the mystery of the Holy Family,
Be present in our daily life, ever drawing us out of our resistance

To calling on you each and every day on the path that pulls
Us through the vortex of time, drawing ever more people
Heavenward, while multiplying the cultivation of the earth

Through which we pass, as pilgrims, bequeathing ever greater
Benefits to those who remain and raising a song of praise,
Ever resounding, ever mounting the reasons for thanksgiving.

Amen.

IMMOBILE

There are those near us, whether our brother or sister in the flesh or not, yet they are a brother or sister in the human family and, therefore, there is a meaning to the plight of illness rendering them almost completely inactive and dependent on the help of others; however, even if that is true, dependence does not mean wanting in good humor and, indeed, what is all the more amazing is being good humored when it is almost impossible to move.

But there are other reasons people cannot move and, one of the most frequent, if largely hidden, is the use of force and confinement. And, even then, there are no doubt a variety of reasons why this is happening: kidnapping; persecution; unjust imprisonment, torture; abuse; forced or any other kind of abortion – for it is always forced on the unborn child.

How is it possible, in this day and age of almost instant communication, surveillance or viral videos and messages, that there are people trapped in the most appalling situations and predicaments: trapped by people like themselves – born and raised and grown up to work?

Whatever happened to human beings becoming human? How amazing is it, then, when husbands and wives, daughters and sons, men and women generally, devote themselves to helping others who, for one reason or another, have been made helpless.

IMMOBILE

Walking down the road
with my wife and parting,

seeing the daffodils and the crocuses
coming up.

Coming in from a bicycle ride
through the park, beside the lake and the swans,
passing passersby with dogs and children,
getting a little wet from a shower,
rejoicing in the sunshine
and calling out that I am back,
checking emails and messages,
making a drink,
walking to and from
the various rooms and seats,
at lunch
with my daughter.

My
brother and sister
have grown still for
reasons of illness,
still but still alive,
one talking but not walking
one neither walking nor talking words
but communicating via signs
and a keyboard.

Living is a unique
experience;

loving, day in and day out,
a modern miracle.

Others
are hidden,
horribly forgotten,
harvested in some way
in the dark.

Will the opening of a door
seem like the resurrection to you?

Will going home
seem like a feverish
apparition?

Will forgiveness
free the spirit from
the walls within
the walls?
Sitting in front of the cross of Christ
I realize that He was immobilized,
pinned to it by nails,
metal, wood and wounds
as unforgiving as deterioration
due to illness and
injustice.

Pray for us

to remember them;

and, remembering them,

I beg you to help them.

COMFORT

This piece was inspired by an excerpt from St. John Henry Newman, who wrote:

"Nothing is so likely to corrupt our hearts, and to seduce us from God, as to surround ourselves with comforts, - to have things our own way, - to be the centre of a sort of world, whether of things animate or inanimate, which minister to us. For then, in turn, we shall depend on them; they will become necessary to us, their very service and adulation will lead us trust ourselves to them, and to idolize them"[10].

On the one hand there are all kinds of comfort that belong to the human condition. Indeed, beginning with those "out-of-home" treats that seemed like nectar to a child and then going on to those times when the answer seemed to be some kind of poetic gyration in a room alone but then, over many years, discovering the breaking of isolation to be like the breaking of an egg – messy in the making but a life out-breaking taking a nowhere going life somewhere even if it was unclear

---

[10] Cited by Fr. Ian Ker, in his book called *Healing The Wound of Humanity: The Spirituality of John Henry Newman*, on pp. 95-96, from *Parochial and Plain Sermons*, 8 vols: *PS* vii. 98.

where. On the other hand there is that ever-present tendency to withdraw: to seek a kind of non-involvement in the day to day reality of life: its gritty difficulties of getting on with each other, helping to occupy the unoccupied or silly children; and then there is prayer, like a constant return to the corner in a boxing ring, ever refreshing and able to return us to the next job of clearing up, the homework check and the evening's activities of one kind or another, whether at home or elsewhere.

Comfort, then, has an array of meanings, almost like an ice-cream eaten or a tender human embrace; but, as we pass through all its different aspects or shades, so perhaps there is one we are still waiting for: the welcome to an eternal home.

COMFORT
comes in a variety
of shapes and sizes:

an invitation to tea,
banana sandwiches,
televised football,
soft sofas – no demands
and no chores.

Growing up to washing-up-work,
a room of my own,
nobody else there –
dancing in isolation.

Working
on a building project that struggles
to pay the bills:

a cigarette, a bacon sandwich,
a cup of tea in a café
on a cold morning's break
from winter-working
on a building's concrete floor,
covered in cardboard
stopping the striking-up-cold,
opening onto the bleak-outside,
blowing-chilly,
starting-a-stomping to stop the pain
rising up the legs.

After
years of traveling
arriving at the stopping point
of marriage and family life:

lying amidst the pillows,
cushions and bedclothes,
exhausted, resting, arrested,
as the clotting in the legs and lungs,
pneumonia and pleurisy,
brings its own way of bringing
down the determination to write

in the basement of a house,
too pressurized to leave,
too full of the fear of failing
the founding of a family
and the shadows from within
forming a barrier without

until,
as if being broken out
of being fixed to finish,
felled, almost uprooted,
freed from finishing,

parted from the work-to-be-grown,

brought to an almost restful close
of striving for the impossible
completion of a book
unfinishable before
the time and the money
ran out further.

Or the tears that roll irretrievably
down the cheeks,
loosening the sobbing,
shoulder slumping, shaking and shuddering
over life's wasted loving,

withering pride's pretence

of being good, noble and generous,

falling into the embrace of being forgiven,
welcomed,
enabled to remain in the house of healing,
hoping, dimly, in the promise of help,
through the arms
of Christ and His Church.

But there is the temptation to sit in the sun,
to read instead of work,
to abandon the children instead of helping,
to reject instead of reconciling,
to recoil instead of encountering,
to remain instead of going

towards the other.

Comfort,
contrary to the dynamism of communion,
is a sedentariness which silts up
until the sin is so completely hidden
it clogs the passage of life.

Uncertainty,
precariousness,

and illness

were insufficient
to turn me to Christ –
I had to be convinced
of sin: of being
a sinner in need of
salvation,

seeking that
eternal
rest.

GUEST POET AND POEM: JAMES SALE

James Sale has been a poet for over 50 years and had 9 collections of poetry published. Most recently his poems have appeared in the UK and USA in many magazines and online forums. In 2017 he won First Prize in the Society of Classical Poets annual competition and in 2019 appeared in New York's Bryant Park and Manhattan's Princeton Club performing live with leading American poets. He is also a regular feature writer on myth and culture for New York's *The Epoch Times*. Currently, James is working on a sequence of English Cantos emulating Dante's Divine Comedy and using the terza rima form[11]:

---

[11] 'Terza rima is a rhyming verse stanza form that consists of an interlocking three-line rhyme scheme. It was first used by the Italian poet Dante Alighieri': https://en.wikipedia.org/wiki/Terza_rima.

progress on the project can be found on James' website located online at https://englishcantos.home.blog.

"COULD I BUT":
An Introduction by the author James Sale

Some years ago I attended a weekend retreat specifically for studying the Psalms and using them as a basis for inspiring and writing poetry. It was a wonderful and energising weekend away with about a dozen people, and it was wholly engrossing to look at the Psalms from a poetical point of view. One of my favourite Psalms has always been Psalm 27.4 and the extraordinary assertion by King David that there is only one thing he would ask of the Lord God. When you consider that he is already a king, and that he is in a unique relationship with God – a man after God's own heart – then what he actually asks for seems almost inconsequential. He could have asked God for power, riches, health or wisdom; indeed, his son Solomon is subsequently endowed with wisdom surpassing that of all other human beings.

But David asks for none of these things: he asks to see "the beauty of the Lord" (and to do so dwelling in His house forever). The beauty – ah! – that's the thing; if but it were a "thing". To see Him as He is, not His back as Moses saw; but that beauty which if it could be seen would entrance one in its sublimity forever: one might never look away, and yet one would never tire. Such is the desire in the heart of King David. And such a vision would by its very and inherent nature purge one through and through – one at last would be clean, as light demolishes all trace of dark.

As I came to write my poem, I noticed how all the other delegates wrote in free verse, but not the sort of structured verse that is in the Psalms. I found that very unsatisfactory, so I set out to do something different. Three tight quatrains (metrical stanzas of 4-lines) using consonantal rhymes in the second and fourth lines (rhymes where the consonants match or nearly match: *lives/love*, or be*low/law*); and following the three primary senses of sight, sound and touch, so that seeing Him would cleanse all my senses, which are the organs of temptation. The result is the conditional poem, Could I But – could I but see, hear and feel, then the new Adam would be re-born.

I hope you enjoy this work.

COULD I BUT

For I know my transgressions,
And my sin is ever before me (Psalm 51.3)

One thing I have asked from the Lord, that I shall seek;
… To behold the beauty of the Lord (Psalm 27.4)

Could I but see that face I'd know
So deep inside me beauty lives,
And all the ugliness I've done
Would be reformed, informed by love.

Could I but hear that voice of His -
Like some bell sounding well below
The walled resistance of my mind -
At last I would obey His law.

Could I but feel His touch on me
My sickness would be swept out clean -
The fever broken - shame flushed free -
And I would be a child again.

Epilogue

This book has wound its way through many changes, delays and rewritings and, indeed, in some ways it is a complete surprise: a book almost from scratch – starting from recent poems and only, very occasionally, taking up a piece written previously.

On reflection, then, what emerges is a dialogue between grace and nature; and, often, nature is what it is because grace has not penetrated its depths and, like the work of a gardener, trimmed its excesses and cultivated its beauty. "Denatured", then, is a particular piece in which, written early on in the life of this collection, the axial drama of this book began to show; and, under its influence, and the influence of the suggestion to extend the book to seven parts, there emerged the section on the "Sacraments" – all of which express the grace-enriched reality of human signs and words.

At the same time, however, there is the influence of prayer even when the subject seems remote, like the use of phones in "Phoneheads", simply because there are so many natural points of contact between the modern condition and an openness to God; indeed, it is as if the very nature of prayer is that it not only grows to be a part of everything we do – but that in spreading into every aspect of our life and activity it is like the presence of a good companion who brings the best out of all of us. In other words it began to make more sense of the contents of the book to consider how, while not automatic at all, the opening to God comes in diverse ways and circumstances and leads to receiving the Sacraments: the outward signs of God's action in our lives – the outward signs which open us up in a new way to the presence of the person of Jesus Christ, our Lord and Saviour. But, gradually, prayer has come to be more explicit as the book has progressed; and, indeed, prompts the realization that there is a common meditation on people's lives that begets both poetry and prayer.

Just, then, as the book as a whole is a kind of coalescence of different impressions and starting points and that collaborating with others introduces an echo of encouragement as well as an opportunity to provide a window on other people's work – so there is the realization that there can be a coming together of what is external with what is internal in the moment of writing. Thus the writing of "Awakening" arose out of both watching and wondering about the growth of seeds while, at the same time, thinking about why God's word can be effectively sent to beget a new beginning in the life of the sinner; and so, in a way, there is a fluidity to the mixture and growth of what makes a piece of writing, whether poem or prose, almost as if there is a crystallization that occurs at a certain moment and that moment is where the writing takes a start.

Perhaps, then, the nuggets of other people's contributions, the mystery of the action of God and the question of giving all contribute, along with the reality of the title being too plain and evoking too explicitly what is already written – to changing the title to *Honest Rust and Gold: A Second Collection of Prose and Poetry*; however, I have to add that discussing the various possibilities and permutations of the title with my family has definitely helped me to come to this conclusion. In other words, what we trash the good Lord makes transparently beautiful; and, indeed, a part of God's work of transforming my life is definitely about doing it through the company and conversation of my wife, family and wider Church community and contacts!

Finally, there is an inevitable tracing, throughout all this, of the writer's journey; and, implicitly, an encouragement to others to either begin or to continue on the path of life! In the midst of this journey is the realization of "unreachability": that there is a point where our efforts end and, in a word, there appears more clearly the helping hand of God. So, whether it is we who have been unreachable, members of our family or friends or, indeed, anyone – there is the mysterious consolation of the Christian Faith that, in reality, no one is beyond the reach of God. And even if we are *tempted to refuse the outstretched hand of the Lord*, may His love prevail over the withdrawal of our hand, grasping us firmly on board the boat bound for heaven:

Look at the love-fire in the light:

the morning brightness amidst the leaves in the trees

telling of beauties still to be told -

continue, if you will, words to unfold

hearts to unfreeze, lives to unleash

through the prayers

still to be prayed.

Amen.

END WORD

JOHN O'BRIEN FRATER AT OFM (FRANCISCAN)

I am a Franciscan friar. I was born in Galway, Ireland. I studied science before I experienced a call. I have worked as a teacher, hospital chaplain and confessor. I got to know Shaun Edwards, the rugby coach, and he brought me to London Wasps[1]. I write on spirituality and mental healing. I am a cancer survivor. A friend of mine from many miles away knew in prayer I was ill and she prayed for me. The operation went well. I survived. I now live in Multyfarnham, Ireland.

Psalm 8 is a beautiful psalm that teaches us God's view of us. It reads:

How great is your name, O Lord our God,
through all the earth!

Your majesty is praised above the heavens;
on the lips of children and of babes
you have found praise to foil your enemy,

---

[1] Cf. .https://www.dailymail.co.uk/sport/rugbyunion/article-492793/Edwards-flies-priest-turned-Wasps-winners.html.

to silence the foe and the rebel.

When I see the heavens, the work of your hands,
the moon and the stars which you arranged,
what is man that you should keep him in mind,
mortal man that you care for him?

Yet you have made him little less than a god;
with glory and honor you crowned him,
gave him power over the works of your hands,
put all things under his feet.

All of them, sheep and cattle,
yes, even the savage beasts,
birds of the air, and fish
that make their way through the waters.

How great is your name, O Lord our God
through all the earth!

The psalm begins with praising God's name in all the earth. All things come from him. The psalmist goes on to speak of the Heavens praising God. When we look at the images brought to us by the Hubble telescope, we see the universe is more vast and mysterious than we ever could imagine. Children have a sense of wonder that we often lose. This sense of wonder leads to praise.

Then the psalmist looks at the human beings that God created. The world outside, the world we see, is vast and complex. The world inside each of us is as vast and complex. Each human being is a mystery. Human beings are not just a collection of chemicals. This part of the psalm is a form of commentary on Genesis 1:27: "So God created mankind in his own image, in the image of God he created them, male and female he created them". In the eyes of God each of us has a unique dignity. Yes, we have fallen from that dignity but in Jesus that dignity is restored. We come to love ourselves as God loves us and we see that others are worthy of that love. Francis' collection shows us that this dignity can be restored and we can live this love in the vicissitudes of daily life.

"How great is your name, O Lord our God,
through all the earth."

www.ingramcontent.com/pod-product-compliance
Lightning Source LLC
Chambersburg PA
CBHW062051080426
42734CB00012B/2607